Journey up the Thames
William Morris and
Modern England

Contents

Acknowledgments

Six acknowledgments are called for in particular. Firstly, my thanks to Jay Derrick for introducing me to the work of Patrick Wright on an enjoyable train journey from Oxford to London. Secondly to Martin Haggerty of the William Morris Society for pointing me to Patrick Keiller's film 'Robinson in Space' which taught me that it is not necessary at all times to be solemn in order to be serious. 'Robinson' turns up at various points in *Journey up the Thames*. Both Wright and Keiller served to validate my own approach to understanding reality through the way things may begin to make sense (or not) across time and space. Thirdly, a general acknowledgement to the William Morris Society of which I am proud to be a member. Their library, lecture programme and newsletters, together with discussions with individual members, have sustained me through a long and complicated writing project. Fourthly, I want to thank Clive Edwards who shared a memorable visit to Kelmscott Manor with me and my elder daughter Annie on 4 September 1991 — the day of the mulberries and the day this writing project began in earnest. Fifthly, the trustees of the Faringdon Collection allowed the use of Maria Spartali's painting of Kelmscott Manor on the front cover. Finally, the book owes a debt to Tony Benn who alerted me many years ago to the deep historical roots of democracy and socialism in England.

I would also like to thank all of those people who have helped me with different aspects of the project. While I would not expect them to agree with what I have to say about either Morris or the communities within which they live and work, I hope that they will all feel that I have treated their contributions to the project in a fair and honourable way. That matters in a society in which people are so often treated with scorn and disdain by journalists, politicians, bureaucrats and business people.

Although this is not intended as a scholarly book, I have referenced all the secondary material I have used in footnotes, for people who want to follow up particular ideas, or simply start an argument with me. In the case of Morris's own writings, I have clearly indicated the source, but without reference to particular editions — there are simply so many. Most of Morris's work is now available in a variety of editions, including a recent CD ROM.

John Payne
Frome, Somerset
January 2000

Introduction

There was no single point at which William Morris entered my consciousness. He was never mentioned at school, unless it was one of the many moments when I was thinking about something else, and as I avoided being a student of English Literature, Art and Design or Victorian social thought, there was no reason for me ever to come across his work. And I hasten to add that I did not grow up in a household with Morris fabrics at the windows or volumes of Carlyle, Ruskin, Marx and Morris on the book-shelves. Yet come across him I did, and what I do know is that, at the age of 21, I spent some of my first salary cheque in a bookshop in Sauchiehall Street in Glasgow on a Nonesuch Press edition of *William Morris's Selected Writings*, edited by G.D.H. Cole. This edition, with its handsome 'Willow' pattern end-papers, contains not only the complete text of *News from Nowhere* but also a good deal of poetry and some of the key lecture and essay texts such as 'How We Live and How We Might Live' which are used extensively in this book. It was 1966.

That little brown book has been a constant companion over the last 34 years. During that period I also learned (as an Open University student and tutor) a lot more about the links between Morris's design work and his social and political beliefs. In addition, I was involved in a wide range of political and community activities which at frequent moments made me despair of the possibility of peaceful social change. They have been years when the labour movement has often seemed to be moving backwards, partly because of the onslaughts of Thatcherism, but partly also because of its own inertia and reluctance to come to terms with a world very different from that inhabited by Marx, Engels and Morris.

This book is neither an attempt to rubbish Morris nor to put him upon a pedestal. In brief, I shall seek to show that many of Morris's essential values, particularly as expressed in *News from Nowhere*, are still relevant to our world today. At the same time, I shall also try to demonstrate ways in which Morris was wrong — both in his predictions about the future and in the political positions he adopted in the 1880s and 1890s. Whatever progress has been made over the past 100 years has been made by democratic socialism operating through parliament and through local government, through the work of the trade unions and other progressive membership organisations. I would hazard a guess that in the twenty-first century, any advances that are made are more likely to come from within the new social movements than from mainstream political parties. There are big problems, some of which Morris would have known about (poverty, inequality, hopelessness), but there are no longer big solutions. At a local level, and in loose alliances at national and international level, people will do what they can to mitigate the worst effects of human kind's enemies: greed, militarism, global capitalism, disease, ethnic tensions, global warming and environmental degradation. As in the nineteenth century, there is scope for pessimism of the intellect, optimism of the will, though at least we now know some of the solutions that do not work ...

The more immediate roots of *Journey up the Thames* come from my years of working in Putney, and my not too successful membership of the South Bank Sailing Club between Putney and Hammersmith, which I describe in chapter one of the book. The project developed from an intense sense of place and its importance in people's lives. From an early stage, it took the journey form from *News from Nowhere*, Morris's utopian novel in which the visitor from the future (Guest) and his guides to Nowhere travel up the river from London to Kelmscott Manor, Morris's house by the river in Oxfordshire. *Journey up the Thames* develops this idea of the journey as a way of looking at how people live in the light of their own concerns and of the ideas and values of William Morris himself.

I did not necessarily go to particular places in search of material on particular themes. Sometimes, this would suggest itself fairly easily. For example, from an early stage I knew that I would probably write about inequality and social division in relation to Oxford, and about the future of the English countryside in the Kelmscott area. Other themes emerged as I explored the towns and villages along the Thames — for example the broad theme of risk at Abingdon or the future of work in Reading. The book grew through the 1990s with large doses of both intuition and serendipity. Meeting real people and listening to real voices seems to me still the most obvious way to write about social reality. Particular events also helped to focus my mind, such as the 350th anniversary of the Putney Debates in 1997 which is the source of chapter three, which appeared (at the suggestion of Peter Hain, MP for Neath but a long-standing Putney resident and activist) in a different form as a Tribune pamphlet in 1997. There is no doubt that the centenary of Morris's death in 1996, the appearance of Fiona MacCarthy's splendid biography of Morris, and the interest aroused by the major exhibition at the Victoria and Albert Museum that year made it easier to interest a publisher. In that same year, the project first acquired some kind of real shape and substance when Tony Coleman, then Leader of Merton Council and now MP for Putney, read an early draft of chapter one and encouraged me to approach the Merton Library Service with a proposal for a publication on 'William Morris and London' as part of Merton's own 1996 celebrations of the life and work of William Morris.

A brief guide to the journey

Chapter One: William Morris and London.

The opening chapter explores London: the dirty, ugly unhealthy city which Morris lived in for much of his life; the utopian 'green' city he imagines in *News from Nowhere*; and the complex, fragmented city of the year 2000. Particular emphasis will be placed on the irony that it was precisely the 'commercial' Victorian city which Morris rails against in his lectures which also provided the basis for the equally 'commercial' success of Morris and Co. The chapter concentrates on four geographical areas of London: Walthamstow, where Morris was born, now an ugly but relatively stable working-class community; Bexleyheath where Morris lived for a number of years at Red House; Merton, where Morris and Co. had their main manufacturing base; the Thames between Hammersmith and Putney. These places can also be understood as starting points for the exploration of social change in twentieth century England.

Chapter Two: Hampton: citizens and subjects.

This chapter explores some of the ambiguities of life in modern England, stuck between England (a nation without an obvious form), Britain (a concept without a future) and Europe (deeply unpopular). These complexities and muddled identities are further complicated by our ambiguous status as 'subjects' of the crown rather than 'citizens' of a modern democracy. Hampton Court Palace and the Hampton Open Air Swimming-Pool are the rather unlikely twin foci of my discussion of these issues. Morris himself represents an important bridge between historical consciousness (love of the past, respect for its art and buildings) and a progressive political agenda which aims to decrease class differences and tackle major social evils such as poverty, ill-health and unemployment. In the book, I shall criticise Morris's own political views and, even more, those who have sought to make of him on the one hand a non-political artist and on the other hand a precursor of orthodox Marxism-Leninism.

Chapter Three: From Putney to Runnymede: a reflection on democracy.

If the flowery meadows of Runnymede are the site most closely identified with the development of democracy in England, it is curious that the most obvious memorials at Runnymede are to American democracy. This chapter links the early stirrings of democracy at Runnymede with the important discussions which took place at St Mary's Church in Putney in 1647, and the shortcomings of both our current English and American versions of democracy. Morris's own views on inequality and the limitations of representative democracy are addressed directly at this point in the book. I shall argue that *News from Nowhere* still has a lot to teach us about how society can be organised as the vehicle for the expression of desire, and how liberty, equality and fraternity are linked.

Chapter Four: Windsor, Eton and Slough

Is it too crude a contrast, between the English standing joke of Slough — the town you never know you have visited until you see the sign saying you're leaving it, Windsor — the profile of its castle one of the few silhouettes which most English people would recognise at once, and Eton — the traditional home of English snobbery and class difference? Maybe, but it is a curious accident of place which finds them located so conveniently near to one another.

Chapter Five: Cookham: a very English village?

This chapter deals with the contrasting attitudes to art, sex and religion of William Morris and the Cookham painter Stanley Spencer. It also deals with some of the questions around the ideas of 'heritage' and 'Englishness', suggesting for example that claiming Spencer as 'English' makes as little sense as regarding Cookham as a 'village'.

Spencer shared none of Morris's instincts for either the commercial or public life, yet in his paintings he expressed that spark in ordinary people which makes them a part of eternity, a part of the essential and ongoing drama of human life, which expresses their equality as human beings. That is there in Morris too. Both men led intensely interesting sex lives, although Spencer seems to have been the more active of the two. Some feminist reservations about Morris are given an airing too.

Chapter Six: Reading and work

The argument in Morris about the proper uses of technology rages still. So what better place to explore the significance of Morris's ideas than England's own Silicon Valley, the high technology industries dominating the M4 corridor? Work is considered in various settings, including high tech industry, professional football and public transport. This is one of several chapters which owes much to my years of reading Raymond Williams, one of the more perceptive social critics of the twentieth century.

I shall emphasise that Morris has been too firmly placed on the Luddite wing of the debate about machine production. He identified the way machinery could replace boring, repetitive labour, as well as producing new forms of it. In a similar way, the new knowledge-based technology of our own second industrial revolution makes significant improvements in working conditions possible, but also produces its own forms of drudgery. Underlying both arguments is the question of 'production for human need or for profit?'

Chapter Seven: Abingdon and risk

Modern life involves risks and insecurities incomparably greater than those known to Victorian England. In the Abingdon area, these include nuclear power and pollution of various kinds, not to mention one of the largest power stations in the UK. The issue of genetic modification, especially in relation to agriculture, appears here too. The evil

Morris identifies in the prose romances may, in the light of twentieth century history, indicate fatal flaws in the make-up of human beings. Are we making, or have we already made, irreversible changes to the climate and environment of planet earth which endanger our survival as a species? To Morris's moral and aesthetic preference for simplicity are added the scientific arguments about ecology. While Morris's views on violent social conflict seem largely irrelevant to 'mainstream' politics, the techniques of direct action are now often used in conflicts about environmental issues, particularly centred on issues such as nuclear power, genetically modified food and road-building.

Chapter Eight: Oxford: unequal to the task?
The inequalities of wealth and poverty, culture, work and risk dominate the central chapters of the book. In the later chapters, the emphasis is upon newer forms of association, community and solidarity which have the potential to produce a happier future than that sketched in the previous chapter. Oxford is an ideal place to begin. On the one hand it is where Morris and his friends formulated a cosy, medievalist, male view of fraternity which he later tried to apply more widely to society. On the other hand it is the modern site of conflict between town and gown (or academia and industry), and of urban risings by an emerging 'underclass' which sees 'society' as something lying over and against them rather than something of which they are an integral part. My view of Oxford incorporates both Morris's own experience of Oxford, the dramatic decline of the car industry in Oxford, and the attempt to find solutions to intractable social problems which will persist well into the new century.

Chapter Nine: Kelmscott and the English countryside
This chapter is located in and around the Cotswold hamlet of Kelmscott, where Morris is buried, and the lovely old

manor house, images of which adorn both the Kelmscott Press edition of *News from Nowhere*, and many other Morris books. Yet this chapter will focus on the realities of life in the countryside today, and what kind of future lies in store for rural people. The crafts are alive and flourishing in the Cotswolds, and yet many of the communities in this part of England have lost touch with their rural roots. They consist predominantly of people who either travel to London and Oxford to work, or older people who have retired to the countryside having made their living in urban settings. I shall argue that heritage is a relative value, and that rural England urgently needs jobs and hope for its young people.

Chapter Ten: Life, the universe and everything: a trip to the source of the Thames

My own narrative differs in one significant aspect from the journey described in *News from Nowhere*: it goes beyond Kelmscott to the landscape he described in *The Earthly Paradise*, four years before first leasing Kelmscott Manor:

What better place than this then could we find
By this sweet stream that knows not of the sea,
That guesses not of the city's misery,
This little stream whose hamlets scarce have names,
This far-off, lonely mother of the Thames?

My own text is a somewhat tongue-in-cheek ramble around the issue of origins and the material and symbolic importance of water in the modern world. It is both a serious conclusion to the book and a reminder that humour is a fundamental way in which human beings deal with the ups-and-downs of everyday life. Humour is serious, some might say. As throughout the book, these discussions will be located in an evoked landscape which is a landscape both of experience and of imagination. To re-imagine our own Englishness can be a way of coming to grips with the drama of the modern world — people's need to feel secure within their own personal and social identity in a way that does not imply the rejection of alternative experience and imagination. A new emphasis on the local is the other side of the coin of globalisation. I argue finally for a tolerance deeply rooted in a sense of who we are and where we come from, but a willingness to work with people very different from ourselves to construct a better world. As my mum used to tell us: 'Leave the world a better place than you found it.' Or as Morris put it: 'To do nothing but grumble and not to act, that is throwing away one's life.'[1]

---

1.   J.M. Mackail, *The life of William Morris*, volume 2, chapter 12 (Longmans, Green and Co, 1899). Mackail's biography is also available on the 'William Morris Collection' CD (ElecBook, eb 0004) which includes most of Morris's writing and illustrations of his design work.

Chapter 1
William Morris and London

Forget six counties overhung with smoke,
Forget the snorting steam and piston stroke,
Forget the spreading of the hideous town;
Think rather of the pack-horse on the down,
And dream of London, small, and white, and clean,
The clear Thames bordered by its gardens green.
(William Morris)

Introduction

William Morris was a necessary failure. Poet, artist, designer, businessman, socialist, weaver and dyer, he tried to do more with his life than most of us ever dream of. We live in a world of specialisms where people define themselves by the job they do, a leisure interest, a family or community role. It is not an age for the polymath. The accusation 'Jack of all Trades, master of none' has often been levelled at Morris. Yet the variety of Morris's endeavours is central to his nature — restless, striving, passionate — and to his views on art and life which stress the moral virtue of craft qualities such as truth to materials and truth to nature rather than aesthetic notions of perfection. It is the spirit of one of Morris's mentors, John Ruskin, who wrote in *The Stones of Venice*: 'You must either make a tool of the creature or a man of him. You cannot make both. Men were not intended to work with the accuracy of tools, to be precise and perfect in all their actions.'

There is little doubt in my mind that Morris's reputation has stayed and grown precisely because his life makes such a good yarn. 'What happens next?' 'Does our hero get his girl?' 'Will the villain pay for his evil deeds?' 'Will Morris win England for socialism and revolution?' The tale is told and retold, much like the romances of Arthur and the Round Table, or the Icelandic sagas which so excited Morris at different periods in his life. Morris's life is full of beginnings — architecture, design, poetry, politics, Iceland. We know the ending. William Morris lies under the extraordinary tomb designed for him by Philip Webb in Kelmscott churchyard in the Cotswolds. And then the myths begin — the careful editing out of any aspect of Morris the family circle doesn't care for, whether it be his cuckolding by Dante Gabriel Rossetti, the exact nature of his relationships with Georgiana Burne-Jones (wife of the Pre-Raphaelite painter Ned, later Sir Edward, Burne-Jones) or London socialite Aglaia Coronio, his socialism, his business methods... There is so much to Morris, so many paths down which to be led astray. Because ultimately it is not the detail of biography which matters, but Morris's creative achievement: his poetry, his designs, the way he both reflects and moulds the important channel of critical thought on art and society which goes from Blake through Ruskin and Carlyle and Edward Carpenter to men as prosaic but as important as Raymond Unwin, the architect of the English Garden City and New Towns movements. In his early years, Unwin had written for Morris's journal, *Commonweal*.[2] Half a century later, in his acceptance speech for the Royal Institute of British Architects Gold Medal in 1937, Unwin summed up the practical influence of the nineteenth century tradition of social and aesthetic criticism:

"One who was privileged to hear the beautiful voice of John Ruskin declaiming against the disorder and degradation resulting from the laissez-faire theories of life; to know William Morris and his work, and to imbibe in his impres-

---

2. See also Colin Ward, 'An old house among new folk: making nowhere somewhere', in (eds) S. Coleman and P. O'Sullivan, *William Morris and News from Nowhere: a vision for our time* (Green Books, 1990), pp.127-9

sionable years the thought and writings of men like James Hinton and Edward Carpenter, could hardly fail to follow after the ideals of a more ordered form of society, and a better planned environment for it, than that which he saw around him in the 'seventies and 'eighties of last century".[3]

William Morris attempted to transcend the shortcomings both of his own life and the England he lived in — harsh, ugly, divided — by projecting his vision of the world as it might be into the future. The result was his utopian novel *News from Nowhere* (1890). In the opening chapters, Morris revisits a much-changed London where money, the essential exchange mechanism which controlled and structured human and social relations in Victorian England, had been abolished, the Houses of Parliament had been turned into a giant dung-hill, and the central parks had been colonised as market gardens and public playgrounds. Later in the novel, the central character Guest, and his guides to Nowhere, embark on a boat journey up the Thames to Kelmscott Manor, the Cotswold house in a Thames-side hamlet which Morris rented jointly for many years with Dante Gabriel Rossetti. It is a symbolic journey of escape and of discovery.

In her 1995 biography of Morris, Fiona MacCarthy emphasised the deep ambivalence of Morris's relationship with London.[4] It is perhaps an ambivalence we all share — is there any other city in the world 'affectionately' known by such a grudging title as 'The Smoke'? As Sir Richard (Lord) Rogers, the architect of the Paris Pompidou Centre and the London Lloyd's Building, said in an interview shortly after becoming a 'working' peer:

"Cities are the places we have to get sorted out. Cities have always been the greatest sources of creativity. But cities are also where we face our most pressing problems,

3. In Walter Creese, *The search for environment: the Garden City before and after* (Yale University Press, 1966) pp.158/9
4. Fiona MacCarthy, *William Morris* (Faber and Faber, 1994)

of poverty and housing and the environment. If we do not get those sorted out we will have the most awful crisis."[5]

On the one hand, London symbolised for Morris the ugliness of nineteenth century England, its commercial greed, the squalor in which most of its inhabitants lived and the enormous disparities of wealth and poverty. On the other hand, William Morris spent most of his adult life in London, apart from a brief period at Red House which Philip Webb built for Morris in Bexley, then in rural Kent, now in suburban London. After leaving Bexley he lived and worked at Queen Square in Bloomsbury, and later in Chiswick. Kelmscott Manor was only intermittently the rural haven of bliss Morris had intended, thanks to Rossetti and his twin addictions to chloral and to the third inhabitant of Kelmscott — Morris's own wife Jane. Indeed, some commentators have suggested that the main purpose of renting Kelmscott Manor was to provide a place where the Jane Morris-Rossetti relationship could play itself out, far from the glare of London life and publicity. In 1879, he wrote in a letter (probably to his lifelong friend Georgiana Burne-Jones): 'Somehow I feel as if there must soon be an end for me of playing at living in the country: a town-bird I am, a master-artisan, if I may claim that latter dignity.' Two years later, in another letter (17 March 1881), he referred to himself less flatteringly as 'a bird of this world-without-end everlasting hole of a London'.[6]

From 1879 Morris divided his life between Kelmscott House, the riverside house in Hammersmith which bears the same name as the manor, and his increasingly successful business ventures at Merton Abbey, on a willow-fringed stretch of the river Wandle just South of

---

5. *New Statesman*, 20 September 1996, pp.28/29
6. For Morris's letters, see Norman Kelvin, *The collected letters of William Morris*, 4 volumes (Princeton University Press, 1984, 1987, 1996 and 1996). Volume 1 covers 1848-80, volume 2 1881-88, volume 3 1889-92, volume 4 1893-96.

Wimbledon, on the south side of Merton High Street. As Fiona MacCarthy puts it: 'London was indeed his city, and he never lost his sense of the London that might be'.[7] In Hammersmith Morris used his own Hammersmith Socialist Society to propagate his socialist ideals and enthusiasms to a hostile world. At Merton Abbey, Morris created not only a business for the design and manufacture of stained glass, furniture, fabrics and wallpaper but also a customer base. And that customer base was precisely the affluent, commercial, metropolitan middle class which Morris loathed. From this deep ambivalence between commercial success and political failure emerge the twin threads that have kept the name of William Morris alive in the century since his death: the Morris who offered the urban middle-class an image of itself formed from the folk memories of rural England; and Morris the socialist activist, campaigning for revolutionary changes in the organisation of society and an end to the oppressive poverty of the workers.

Morris and Walthamstow

When William Morris was born in Walthamstow in 1834, it was a rural village in the Essex countryside. The family home had views across the river Lea to Epping Forest in the distance. In later years, Morris remembered the scent of the may-blossom and balm, and the succulent dark blue plums that grew on the kitchen garden wall. Today, little is left of the Walthamstow Morris knew as a child. It is now a predominantly working-class community in northeast London. Often it seems like the last outpost of a traditional 'respectable' working-class way of life which gave way years ago in much of London to the fractured uncertainties of post-industrial society. Ironically the rural past

---

7.   *MacCarthy*, p.112

16

of Walthamstow is still remembered in the name of the borough (Waltham Forest) much as London's East End goes under the rural title of Tower Hamlets. Such points are relevant to Morris in so far as the folksy ruralism of *News from Nowhere* plays counterpoint to Morris's day-to-day life as London businessman and socialist.

Morris's father commuted by carriage to his job in the City. Nowadays, much of the commuter activity is centred on Walthamstow's position as the north-eastern terminus of the Victoria line, which before the opening of the Jubilee line extension, was always the fastest and most efficient artery of London's decaying Underground system. Morning and evening, the population of Walthamstow is swollen by Essex man and Essex woman in their sharp suits, reading *The Times* and *The Evening Standard* or trashy novels, their skin tanned from holidays in the Canary Islands or the Aegean Islands or a hasty visit to the sunbed at the local Leisure Centre. Between morning and evening rush-hours, Walthamstow goes about its own business in its own way, full of inconsequential chatter, clutter and neighbourliness. With its rows of little, anonymous terrace houses hiding behind net curtains, Walthamstow always feels more like the East End of the television soap than most of the East End itself — Bethnal Green, Stepney, Bow all pulverised by wartime bombing, post-war redevelopment, tower blocks, social dislocation and friction between white locals and Bengali and Bangla Deshi newcomers.

Morris would be both fascinated and horrified by Walthamstow today. He would hate the unpretentious, ordinary ugliness of its houses, the tackiness of so many of the goods on sale in shops and market-stalls (Morris exhorted people to have nothing in their homes which was neither beautiful nor useful — most of the goods on display are neither). Yet I cannot help feeling that he would have enjoyed the cheerful exuberance of the crowded pedestrianised street market that dominates the centre of Walthamstow, where not just goods and money change

17

hands, but friendships are daily renewed, gossip shared, the nagging little problems of daily life brought a little closer to resolution or acceptance. Morris would have noticed the healthy bodies, the bright clothes, so different from the pallid, unhealthy faces he discovered when he first ventured into working-class districts of London in the 1880s on his socialist voyages of discovery.

Happiness was, after all, important to Morris. Characteristically, he related it to work, and pride in work. From pleasure in labour grew real art. Maybe! I prefer to emphasise Morris and skill. Morris was a skilled man but also an amateur. Skill for Morris did not mean perfection, but an object produced with some care or thought, which would carry out its job worthily and without constant need of replacement. Work fills less and less of human life. We work shorter hours and shorter working lives, not to mention the scourge of compulsory idleness which we call unemployment. The happiest people I know are those who have an opportunity to practise their skills, whether in paid or voluntary or do-it-yourself work, in a factory or office, or at home, as work or leisure. A lot of *News from Nowhere* is about skills and about the rediscovery of what we might term the 'simple pleasures' of domestic, day-to-day life; neither exceptional nor exciting; unpredictable but within a known range of predictability. Yes, I believe Morris would feel happy in Walthamstow, and hopefully proud to find a William Morris Gallery in the family home, Water House, at the heart of a well laid-out and carefully tended local park.

As is so often the case with Morris, it is his absolutism which causes the problems. It must be real art or phoney art, it is beautiful or it is ugly, it is socialist or it is reactionary nonsense. In political terms, Morris found the gradualism and incompleteness of change as expressed in the democratic institutions of parliamentary democracy intensely irritating. Morris swallowed Marxism not because he had studied it in any depth but because it gave him pat answers with which to inspire his comrades and bully his opponents. There is political thought in Morris, as Edward Thompson sought to show in his monumental *William Morris*.[8] Thompson, a Marxist who was in the process of slackening his ties with the British Communist Party, emphasises Morris's Marxism which was central to the split within the Social Democratic Federation in the 1880s and the setting up of the Socialist League as the 'vehicle' for Morris's own political leadership. He discounts Morris's Anarchist sympathies which eventually enabled the Anarchists to take over and destroy the Socialist League and its journal *Commonweal*, leaving Morris with only the security of family and friends in the cosy little Hammersmith Socialist Society. Neither the Anarchist or Marxist versions of the revolution were to take place in England.

In retrospect, it is unsurprising that Morris's increasingly exhausting and schismatic politicking in the late 1880s coincides precisely with the writing of his glorious political legacy — *News from Nowhere*, first published in 1890 in *Commonweal*.

The rediscovery of the material and domestic as sources of human happiness and fulfilment; free and open sexual relationships; the importance, too, of relationships based on friendship and comradeship; a new and gentler partnership between human beings and the natural environment; the reconciliation of town and countryside; a social system focused on the redistribution of wealth rather than its concentration in a small number of bank accounts; these are the themes which mark out Morris's ongoing importance as a social and political thinker for the twenty first century. These are the subjects that continue to inspire the young and draw them into political commitment, rather than the gaunt message that 'the change'

---

8. E.P. Thompson, *William Morris: romantic to revolutionary* (1955, revised edition, Pantheon Books, 1976)

(the overthrow of capitalism) can only be achieved by violent conflict and upheaval. The 'short twentieth century' (in Eric Hobsbawm's memorable phrase) has taught us that down that route lies an escalation of human suffering rather than its alleviation.

Morris and Bexleyheath

The London Borough of Bexley is prime suburbia with large tracts of semi-detached houses interrupted by occasional concentrations of public housing, pleasant open spaces and noisy, foul-smelling motorways flowing towards Kent and Europe. At the start of the new century, Edward Heath, Conservative Prime Minister in the 1970s, is still the MP for Old Bexley, as he has been since anyone in the borough can remember. One wonders if he is glad to be living under a Labour government which is positive over relations with the European Union, and certainly does not have the xenophobic knee-jerk reactions of many of his younger colleagues on the Tory side of the House.

If Sir Edward is the acceptable face of Conservatism in these parts, its unacceptable face was surely the British National Party's bookshop in Welling High Street, a centre of fascist agitation for years and the focus for many anti-racist demonstrations. Racism is strong in the borough for reasons which are not immediately apparent: not far away in Well Hall Road is the site of the murder of Stephen Lawrence, a young black man killed by white thugs who have repeatedly managed to evade justice with the help of a police force which is, at best, incompetent and at worst, itself implicated in the racism it is supposed to help combat. A BBC opinion poll in the wake of an enquiry into police handling of the affair in 1998 showed that one-in-seven Londoners now have no trust at all in the Metropolitan Police, while half have less trust than before. A 1999 report concluded that the 'Met' was institutionally racist. The case did little for the international reputation of London. Nelson Mandela, President of South Africa, made a very public call on the Lawrence family while on a visit to London.

It is not immediately obvious why Morris chose Bexleyheath to set up home at the start of his marriage to Jane Burden. The site for Red House had already been chosen before their wedding in 1859 and the young couple were to live there from 1860 until 1865. Most likely Morris identified his own youthful enthusiasm for the Arthurian legends and the fellowship of the Round Table with Chaucer's jolly, sociable pilgrims wending their way from the Tabard Inn in Southwark, down the Old Kent Road and along the Roman Watling Street which runs straight and true up Shooter's Hill and across Blackheath towards Canterbury.[9] The garden porch is certainly called 'The Pilgrim's Rest'. Ted Hollamby, who lived at Red House from 1952 until his death in 1999, liked to point as well to the Kentish horse on the weather-vane. This reflects another aspect of Kent — 'rebellious Kent' — which was to become very close to Morris's concerns two decades later. As I describe in chapter three, it was at Blackheath that the men and women of Kent gathered to present their case to the King during the 1381 Peasants' Revolt, which Morris describes in his *A Dream of John Ball*. The relationship between the importance of fellowship for the younger Morris and struggle for the older Morris is significant. As Edward Thompson showed in *The Making of the English Working Class*, the nineteenth century English working class was defined by its very struggle to assert the rights of ordinary people against the moral vacuum at the heart of the capitalist system. It was a class created by capitalism for the purposes of profit but which soon set about erecting its own organisations and institutions to defend its own interests.[10]

Morris would recognise the little row of Hog's Hole cot-

---

9. See Edward Hollamby, *Red House* (Phaidon Press, 1991)
10. E.P. Thompson, *The making of the English working class* (Pelican, 1968)

21

tages which still stand at a curious angle to the modern road, and which were, in the nineteenth century, the heart of the tiny hamlet of Upton. There is a flourishing walnut tree outside, shading both cottages and roads. Apart from the original brick wall, the present owners have allowed a range of trees to grow around the perimeter of the gardens, emphasising the timeless qualities of the red-brick building with its steep barn-like roofs. When I visited Red House with friends in 1998, we were welcomed by Ted Hollamby. He believed that the well was the 'centre of Red House', firstly because it was the house's water supply and secondly because the well, with its wooden seat round, is the natural place to sit and gossip, the focus of the good fellowship which Morris wished to stimulate among his friends. In his last years, Morris took up the symbolic importance of water again in the prose romance of *The Well at the World's End*. In a similar way, I shall return to the central role of water in human culture, the primary resource for people everywhere, at the end of this book. And of course the Thames runs through this book as its unifying thread.

The sense of fellowship was very real on the day of my own visit, for a party of Ted Hollamby's old colleagues from Lambeth, where he was Borough Architect for many years, had come to visit Red House. As he talked of Morris and the dream world of Arthurian legend, the bees buzzed happily among the brightly-coloured, old-fashioned English flowers; the breeze sighed gently in the trees and rippled across the grass. An urban fox crossed swiftly in the sunshine in front of us. That early dream-world of Morris was a world 'uncontaminated by "real" history', as Ted Hollamby put it, so different from the utopia of *News from Nowhere* which is only achieved as the end-result of the bitter class struggle predicted by Karl Marx and taken up by Morris's Socialist League. Beyond the gates there is work still to be done — the London Borough of Bexley...

There are lines and traditions in architecture. In 1936

Nikolaus Pevsner published his classic study *Pioneers of Modern Design*.[11] Morris is identified as the forerunner of modern, rational design, and in that tradition his collaboration with the architect Philip Webb at Red House surely takes pride of place. For all its prettiness, Red House is a practical house, not (in Le Corbusier's phrase) a 'machine for living in' but certainly a series of sensible, clearly organised living spaces which are expressed in the external form of the house. Morris and Webb were not trying, in Pevsner's words, to 'imitate palaces'. If Red House is about the fellowship of the few, it points forward to a modern architecture which is about the fellowship of the many. As an architectural student in the '30s, Ted Hollamby told us he wanted "an architecture for the people, for ordinary people". And again the lines are clear, from Morris and the Arts and Crafts movement, to the Garden City, the inter-war public housing estates and later suburban estates such as the London County Council's Alton estate in Roehampton. This estate sought to provide the survivors of the London blitz with high quality housing in an idyllic setting between Wimbledon Common, Putney Heath and Richmond Park, an area which had been reserved previously for the mansions of the very rich. And there are individual buildings too which reflect this ideal of a social architecture. In London there is the Finsbury Health Centre. In Barcelona there is Josep-Lluis Sert's TB clinic, built in the middle of the Spanish Civil War and setting out in unambiguous terms the social priorities of the Republican government.

Red House has a future as well as a past. There is a 'Friends of Red House' group, and it is likely that eventually a Trust will be set up to secure the future of the house as a family home — which it has always been — but also as a building accessible to members of the public. Part of

---

11. Nikolaus Pevsner, *Pioneers of modern design: from William Morris to Walter Gropius* (1936, revised edition, Penguin Books, 1974)

that access is about protecting Morris's memory from what one might call the 'National Trust norm' of the 'great house'. Red House is a very great house indeed, but it also reminds visitors that in art and architecture, just as in our individual and collective lives, there is a social purpose.

Morris and Merton

Morris hated Merton when he first saw it, describing it as 'woeful beyond conception',[12] but gradually warmed to it, especially the 'pretty little Wandle.'[13] Merton Abbey lies beside the Wandle, which rises at Carshalton and flows into the Thames at Wandsworth. Pretty it is, but the Wandle once played a dramatic role in the early industrial history of England, at one time boasting more mills per mile than any other river in England. The industries of Merton included flour- and snuff-milling, leather, copper and iron, as well as the calico-printing for which the area is best known. The water not only drove the machinery but provided a reliable source of clean water for bleaching and printing. Arriving here in 1881, Morris and Co. occupied a site on the south side of Merton High Street (now part of Sainsbury's Savacentre) continuously until 1940, nearly half a century after Morris's death. During this period the company revolutionised the history of English design, inspired the Arts and Crafts Movement, and transformed the way people thought about the decoration and use of their homes.

There was certainly a branch of the Social Democratic Federation (from 1884 the Socialist League) at Merton Abbey in the 1880s, as well as a circulating library. But in other respects, there were more similarities than differences

12. MacCarthy, p.431
13. Letter to Jane Morris, 19 March 1881

between working conditions at Merton Abbey and other Victorian workplaces. Morris made little attempt to flout the conventions of capitalism, especially in relation to disparities of pay between management and operatives, or the sexual division of labour between 'men's work' and 'women's work'. He wrote to Georgiana Burne-Jones on 1 June 1884:

> It seems to me that the utmost I could do would be little enough, nor should I feel much satisfaction in thinking that a very small knot of working-people were somewhat better off amidst the great ocean of economic slavery.

Charles Harvey and Jon Press[14] have added to our understanding of Morris by emphasising the success of Morris and Co. as a rather typical medium-sized Victorian enterprise which was highly successful in creating a market for household furnishings of an 'artistic' variety, and selling a range of goods at competitive prices.

Modern visitors to the site may be puzzled. To the north is the consumer palace of the Savacentre. Across a modern road (Merantum Way) lies an enormous untidy car-park, and huddled by the river in the far corner a nondescript collection of timber and brick buildings announce Merton Abbey Mills. This is not the site of Morris and Co., but is the site of the first calico-printing works at Merton, established in 1724. From 1902-72 the site was used by Liberty and Co. It is now part museum and heritage centre, part craft workshops and market. Here the modern equivalents of Morris's mediaeval craftsmen sell pottery, jewelry, clothes, fabrics and books to a predominantly young and rootless public. There is even a William Morris pub on the river-bank, neatly defying the prosaic details of local history. And back across the busy road is the enormous Sainsbury's Savacentre — the reverse image of the craft stalls across the other side of the road.

---

14. Charles Harvey and Jon Press, *William Morris: design and enterprise in Victorian Britain* (Manchester University Press, 1991)

Is it merely a class divide — the working class buying a range of pre-packed standardised commodities on one side of the road, the middle class buying its luxury arty-crafty products on the other side? I think not. Isn't it rather that very similar people are expressing different aspects of their own lives as they buy their necessities of daily life at Sainsbury's and the objects to beautify their bodies and homes at the Craft Market? Morris did, after all, admit both the useful and the beautiful into his ideal home. His favourite room in any house he lived in was the kitchen. Morris is one of the few eminent Victorian men of whom we can say with certainty that he knew how to cook for himself and others!

The current London Borough of Merton is a microcosm of many of the themes which emerge from a reading of Morris and continue to be relevant one hundred years later. On its north-western fringes lies Wimbledon Common, the site of one of the great, successful struggles of the nineteenth century between power and privilege and the ordinary people of London. The Spencer family, who had acquired ownership of what had once been common land, were determined to develop the area for housing. They lost, and the people won. The Common was returned to its original status with an elected Board of Conservators to retain and manage the land for common use. Ironically, the areas bordering onto the Common, in and around Wimbledon Village, have become the home of a new sort of privilege, based not on a very few people owning enormous wealth but on significant numbers of people having at their disposal wealth far beyond the reach of the majority — the sorts of people who live in the sprawling council estates stretching south of Wimbledon towards Sutton and Carshalton. These estates, with their high and linked rates of unemployment, petty crime and an absence of dignity and aspiration for many of their residents, are the other side of the coin to pretty Wimbledon with its boutiques and wine bars, its riding stables and fancy shops.

If access to the countryside and disparities of wealth were both important concerns for Morris, a third theme which spans the century between his death and the present is the environment. The Wandle flows through the whole length of the borough of Merton, meandering past disused factories and brand new warehouses, past supermarkets and back gardens, through parks and gardens. How Morris would have loved the Wilderness Island Nature Reserve, quaintly sandwiched between the river and a railway junction at Carshalton, with its profusion of trees and flowers and birds and butterflies, an urban jungle of the authentic variety! The willows lining the quiet eddies and backwaters as the Wandle flows through Morden Hall Park are a Morris motif which can bear the traveller down to Putney and Hammersmith and far beyond to Kelmscott Manor and the upper reaches of the Thames. Even in Wandsworth, the local council are reclaiming the canalised sections of the Wandle, planting and landscaping using wild flowers and native tree species. A primary school near the mouth of the river is powered by electricity from a tidal generator. Small boys and girls are once more to be seen hanging over bridges with their fishing lines.

How has this new concern for the relationship between human beings and their natural environment been achieved? By a mixture of voluntary activity linked to a new awareness by local government that the environment is now a political issue. Does Morris have anything to say on this? Well, part of the legacy that Morris has handed down to modern England is the Society for the Protection of Ancient Buildings. It is an excellent example of what can be achieved by a voluntary pressure-group of well-intentioned citizens. And in his final years, Morris himself was beginning to move in this direction of linked government-citizen action, cautiously embracing some of the gains of the new-style local government. In a lecture in 1893 to his own Hammersmith Socialist Society, he wrote:

> The London County Council, for instance, is not merely a more useful body for the administration of public business than the Metropolitan Board of Works was: it is instinct with a different spirit; and even its general intention to be of use to the citizens and to heed their wishes, has in it a promise of better days, and has already done something to raise the dignity of life in London amongst a certain part of the population, and down to certain classes. Again, who can quarrel with the attempts to relieve the sordidness of civilized town life by the public acquirement of parks and other open spaces, planting of trees, establishment of free libraries and the like? It is sensible and right for the public to push for the attainment of such gains; but we all know very well that their advantages are very unequally distributed, that they are gains rather for certain portions of the middle-classes than for working people.

Significantly, this essay was reprinted as a Fabian Society tract in 1903,[15] a clear sign that the struggle for the Morris inheritance was already underway. This brave new world of environmental concern is, of course, not just a spin-off of the heritage industry. For Morris as for modern environmentalists, heritage was important because it reminds us of values other than those concerned with the grind of daily life — making a living, sustaining relationships, getting by as best we can. Morris correctly identified that these issues would continue to preoccupy what he termed 'working people' and prevent them from enjoying to the full the improvements of well-intentioned politicians and local government officers.

It is deeply ironical that the kind of voluntary involvement in setting new standards for environmental concern at a local level has coincided with the last twenty years of the century when central government has waged war on local government of all kinds. But there is an irony within an irony. The abolition of the Greater London Council and the Inner London Education Authority has placed much

---

15. William Morris, *Communism* (Fabian tract 113, Fabian Society, March 1903)

28

greater powers in the hands of the London borough councils. Along with that there has been a sea change in public attitudes, with people no longer prepared to leave everything to government action alone to make the improvements they see as necessary in their daily lives. Merton has its own Going for Green project in Mitcham — a hopeful and lively initiative to link citizen concerns with local government action. If conflict and centralisation have been the guiding themes of the end of the twentieth century, partnership and local democracy, with the implied threat of direct action, will surely be the presiding themes of the new century.

* * *

Under the road between the Savacentre and the Merton Abbey Mills are the recently excavated remains of the mediaeval chapter-house of Merton Abbey. In this unlikely setting, just twelve feet below the rumble of traffic, as part of the 1996 Merton Arts festival, Gerry Nowicki's *The Dream Factory* was performed, a play about the life and times of William Morris. In this play, Morris is an old man forced to look back on the events of his life: its achievements and its failures; its public triumphs and its private humiliations; his childhood in Walthamstow; his schooling at Marlborough; the happy, mediaevalising student days in Oxford; the difficulties of his marriage; the success of his business ventures; his daughters; his politics; loss and betrayal. Through the play runs the complex symbol of the River of Fire. The source is a lecture Morris gave in 1881 entitled *The Prospects of Architecture*:

> For between us and that which is to be, if art is not to perish utterly, there is something alive and devouring; something as it were a river of fire that will put all that tries (sic) to swim across to a hard proof indeed, and scare from the plunge every soul that is not made fearless by desire of truth and insight of the happy days to come beyond.

It is as if Morris, aware that the changes he wanted to see in art, in society and politics were unlikely to take place in his lifetime, is working his way towards a psychological solution, a cataclysmic act which would somehow magically move things forward from 'how things are' to 'how they might be'. In a letter written to Robert Thomson on 28 July 1884, he is explicit about the violent nature of change: 'we must not say "We must drop our purpose rather than carry it across the river of violence"'. But by then he had discovered Marx and class conflict. That idea of 'the change' and how it might come about is central to *News from Nowhere*.

It has often been pointed out (usually approvingly) that the unique characteristic of Morris's Utopia is that it contains a view of how Utopia is to be achieved. The difficulty of this approach to *News from Nowhere* is the simple fact that it didn't happen, Morris was wrong: revolutions more often produce dystopia rather than utopia. Society has moved on and changed, for better and for worse. Some of those changes have been achieved by means of the parliamentary democracy which Morris despised and rejected. Much more has been achieved by the sheer power of capitalism to continually re-invent itself, by revolutions in technology and our ability to control the natural world. Yet just as insistently, the Morris questions creep back: yes, we were brought up to believe that we control the natural world, but is it not now spinning madly beyond our control? How should we relate to the natural environment? How should we live, and work? What about happiness? What about men and women, and their relationships?

Our uncertainties are partly a result of the loss of faith in both religion and science and the philosophies they promoted. But there are also more compelling reasons for turning back to Morris. All over the world, not just in England, disparities of wealth and poverty are again increasing. In our own country, the abandonment of the post-war settlement of the Welfare State and the mixed economy have produced the paradox that the years of Conservative governments from 1979 to 1987 have made Morris seem relevant again. Not his naive theory of revolution, but the questions he asks and the way he frames them, the moral repugnance which so many of us share at the gross inequalities of wealth and poverty in our society, and the practical consequences of inequality — crime, vandalism and social dislocation.

From Putney to Hammersmith with William Morris

The loveliest stretch of the Thames in London, the sprawling reach that stretches from Putney to Hammersmith, is well-known to millions of people who have never visited it as the first stage of the annual Oxford-Cambridge Boat Race. When the Guest is rowed out from the shore at Hammersmith for an early morning bathe in the Thames (we are in *Nowhere* land again), it is unclear whether it is upstream towards Chiswick and Barnes or downstream towards Putney. My imagination leaves no space for doubt — it must have been Putney. The north bank is thickly populated with flats and old warehouses as far as the Fulham Football Club (itself due for redevelopment) where housing gives way to the great London plane-trees and gardens of Bishop's Park. The palace of the Bishops of London lies a little back from the river. That is the Middlesex side of the river on Boat Race Day; on every other day it is the Fulham side.

On the Surrey (Putney) side the meadows of Barn Elms which Morris knew and loved have given way to reservoirs and poplar-lined playing fields. The reservoirs are now redundant, and one of London's better planning schemes is changing them into a mixed development of houses, flats and a nature reserve to accommodate the large numbers of fowl which have come to regard the reservoirs as their natural breeding-ground. Between the Beverley Brook and Putney Bridge, the boat houses of the rowing

31

clubs create a timeless scene of alternate calm and frenetic activity. Despite the Thames Barrier and the best efforts of Putney Members of Parliament, the river is still allowed to flow over onto the Embankment at exceptionally high tides in spring and autumn. Occasionally an unwary soul still leaves a car on the slipway beneath Putney Bridge and returns to find it floating away on the flood tide.

On a quiet summer's morning, when the calm, grey waters of the Thames are disturbed only by the earliest of early morning scullers or a lonesome, swooping cormorant, it is easy to imagine the scene as Morris describes it at the opening of *News from Nowhere*:

> Both shores had a line of very pretty houses, low and not large, standing back a little way from the river; they were mostly built of red brick and roofed with tiles, and looked, above all, comfortable, and as if they were, so to say, alive and sympathetic with the life of the dwellers in them. There was a continuous garden in front of them, going down to the water's edge, in which the flowers were now blooming luxuriantly, and sending delicious waves of summer scent over the eddying stream. Behind the houses, I could see great trees rising, mostly planes, and looking down the water there were the reaches towards Putney, almost as if they were a lake with a forest shore, so thick were the big trees.

'Comfortable'. Yes, that is a very Putney word. The little terraces of red-brick houses stretching up from the river, that sense of a village which has survived the onslaught of London. I think I fell for Putney on my first visit, walking over the bridge from Fulham, on my way to a job interview on the Putney side. I knew I would always want to come back. For years I worked in Putney and coveted the river, and eventually found what I thought I wanted — membership of a Sailing Club on that very same stretch of water. I had taken on too much. It is one thing to learn to sail on an old chalk pit lake, it is quite another to deal with the Thames tides, the competing traffic of rowers and Thames launches and pleasure cruisers, the surge of flotsam and jetsam which comes upstream on every tide. I think I spent more time in the river than on it. It is unpleasant, cold, smelly and positively dangerous when a motorboat or a great log festooned with rusty nails is bearing down on you, as you struggle to upturn a capsized sailing dinghy.

If my performance on the water was less than spectacular, it did not diminish my affection for the sights and sounds of the river. Aircraft heading west for Heathrow, walkers and dogs on the tow-path which goes all the way from Putney to Oxford, that characteristic boat-club sound of metal wires and shackles jangling contentedly against each other, the wind in the Barn Elms poplars, the glow of a midsummer London twilight falling upon the river. It is blowing up for rain from the South-West but the sky is still streaked with red over towards Hammersmith. The Thames at low tide is a glowing mirror reflecting the lights of the riverside flats upstream on the Hammersmith bank, the pubs and boathouses of Putney Embankment downstream.

Sail or steam, handicraft or factory production, pen or word-processor: what is appropriate technology? The question is framed in a modern way, but is still a Morris question. Morris made it clear that there were boring repetitive processes that might well be replaced by machine. He wanted all work to be creative and fulfilling. So would he have been thrilled by the technology of the second industrial revolution, of computer-driven machines, of word-processors, of information flashed effortlessly around the globe? Obviously, yes, but in order to answer that question it must be placed against another question — that of purpose. Our society, more than any other, plays fast and loose with the land we live on; vast areas of the world have been laid waste to extract natural resources to make goods we buy not because we need them but because we have money in our pockets and shopping has become a major leisure industry. Obesity is a major health problem in the richest nations of the world. Putney has its supermarkets and its shopping mall, as do Merton and Walthamstow, as does any other place in the industrialised world. And those outside the magic circle of growth and wealth — the unemployed and homeless in London, the dispossessed of the poor countries of Africa and Latin America — are filled with an angry, impotent envy which must one day threaten the fragile world order we have.

At the end of the day, Morris was right about inequality even if he got it wrong about revolution. We cannot have society or community, love or fellowship, locally, nationally or globally, if we have inequality. For Morris, that translated itself into the socialist question — how could the great majority represented by the nineteenth century urban working class take power and run society for the benefit of all its members? For many of us at the beginning of the twenty-first century, living in a more complex and fractured society, it is the ecological question too: how can we live in harmony with nature, so that the work we do, the goods we buy and use, the leisure we enjoy, can contribute to the total happiness of human kind rather than our own good at the expense of others? We ask not for a life of wealth and luxury (how many of us in our heart of hearts really want to win the National Lottery?) but for a decent life. As Morris wrote in his 1887 Hammersmith lecture *How we live and how we might live*:

> I will now let my claims for a decent life stand as I have made them. To sum them up in brief, they are: First a healthy body; second, an active mind in sympathy with the past, the present and the future; thirdly, occupation fit for a healthy body and an active mind; and fourthly, a beautiful world to live in.

Nowhere remains the country of all our hearts.

Chapter 2
Hampton: citizens and subjects

"I swim at 6.00 am every morning and it sets me up for the day." (a regular at Hampton Pool)

Such duty as the subject owes the prince,
Even such a woman owest to her husband
(Shakespeare, *The Taming of the Shrew*, V.2)

"A short swim, neighbour, but perhaps you find the water cold this morning, after your journey. Shall I put you ashore at once, or would you like to go down to Putney before breakfast?"
(William Morris, *News from Nowhere*, chapter two, A Morning Bath)

Of communities

I first saw Hampton Court on a mild February day some twenty years ago. In those days the Inner London Education Authority had a small conference centre on Raven's Ait, an island in the Thames just west of Kingston-upon-Thames. We were ferried over to the island on a dark, stormy Friday night, but by Sunday the storm had blown itself out, and the micro-climate of the south-western suburbs of London was tugging us towards Spring. On the Sunday morning we walked across the extensive parkland which stretches between Kingston and Hampton Court, filling the loop between the Thames and the straight road which joins the two places and divides Hampton Court from Bushey Park. It was lovely beyond belief, the crowd of red-brick chimneys clustered above the older part of Henry VIII's palace, the classical façade facing the formal gardens with their tightly clipped conical yew trees which cast long shadows even at midday across the even greensward, The dark green of the tightly coiled bunches of mistletoe in the tall trees of the park was offset by the fuzzy orange of the willows alongside the semi-circular waterway that surrounds the formal garden. Within the walled gardens the first crocuses were peeping through the grass, the camellias were in their full glory.

The thrill of that first visit to Hampton Court has stayed with me, supplemented by frequent visits to the Maze with my children, although my own knowledge of the Maze does not extend much beyond the gate. As for many parents, the Maze at Hampton Court was an excuse for a quiet quarter of an hour on a park bench, lulled by the not so distant screams of excitement issuing from behind the dusty hedges. But there is another Hampton, which I discovered quite by chance. In Wandsworth, where the Thames used to be closely lined with busy wharves, and is now lined by the flats of the well-to-do City types attracted first by the zero Poll Tax and now the low rates of Council Tax, we had a spot of local bother about a swimming-pool. Like many other open-air swimming pools built during the inter-war years when movements as diverse as the Hitler Youth, the Boy Scouts and the sandal-wearing, Esperanto-speaking vegetarians of Letchworth Garden City praised the virtues of fresh air and exercise, the pool in King George's Park in Wandsworth had hit hard times. Necessary repairs and improvements had not been carried out, and facilities were very poor compared to the newer, heated indoor pools in the borough. The local council first tried to shift responsibility onto the private sector by employing a private contractor to run the pool, now renamed the 'Big Splash.' After they had failed to make a profit from it, the council resolved to close the pool and redevelop it as an indoor centre for tennis and bowls. A group quickly formed to oppose the closure of the pool.

At the Public Enquiry, I argued that 'There is a lot of mention in the evidence presented by Wandsworth Council about trees and views, but precious little about people.

And in particular about what kind of people use open-air swimming-pools and how they use them, and what kind of people use indoor sports facilities'. I quoted evidence from North Hertfordshire, where the Conservative council had added an indoor pool to the outdoor pool in Hitchin, rather than simply closing it. They had discovered that older people, unemployed people and the families of manual workers were more likely to use open-air than covered pools. While better-off people squeezed a quick trip to the indoor pool into a busy work and family schedule, the less well-off were more likely to come for a whole afternoon, or even a day, bringing picnics and treating the experience much more like a day at the seaside. I concluded that 'a visit to an open-air swimming-pool close to their homes represents for many people on limited budgets the best value-for-money in recreation.' The pay-and-play philosophy which underlay Wandsworth's recreation policy was bogus, I added, because people had widely differing abilities to pay.

In the event, the inspectors found against Wandsworth Council, not on the kind of social grounds that the Big Splash Action Group had been putting forward, but because the new building constituted an intrusion into the park which is privileged 'Metropolitan Open Space.' I still have a photo on my wall marking this famous 'victory'. But of course Wandsworth Council had no intention of re-opening the pool which eventually became all-weather pitches for activities such as five-a-side football. They are a hard council to beat.

During the Big Splash campaign, I had occasion to visit a number of other open-air pools in the London area. The one I had never been to was the heated pool at Hampton, famous for its Christmas Day swims when up to one thousand people pass through the water on a single day. On 22 March 1998 I set out for an 'official' visit to Hampton Court Palace via the rather unusual route of Hampton open-air swimming-pool. Spring was in the air: the previous day I had been to the wedding of some friends in

Esher: the bride, with red roses and yellow freesias around her head and a hand-embroidered cross-stitch girdle, had been a Morris picture. There was renewal too, in the way they managed to refresh the rituals of marriage by promising not only to love and respect one another but also to love and care for their child.

I swim and talk to a man in the water about the pool — he says it's lovely on a January morning when the temperature is –6°C. The Duty manager, Danny Ashley, responds to my previously unannounced interest in his pool by buying me a coffee at the Flippers café on the roof. The place itself is nothing, compared for example to the 1930s Art Deco splendours of some of the better known lidos — a rather nondescript brick building and a rigidly rectangular swimming-pool which looks as if it may need some money spent on it soon. But some 30 people are swimming and there is a steady stream of coming and going in the car-park. The economics of heated open-air pools are horrendous, and Danny explains to me that the café and the gym help to keep the pool going during the winter months. But they had recognised that the days of unheated outdoor pools in the English climate were probably numbered, and that heating was crucial to their success. There is talk of sinking their own bore-hole to cut the cost of refilling the pool with water, following the example of Oliver Cromwell who, during his residency at Hampton Court, had several fish ponds dug in what is now Bushey Park.

People come to the pool from quite a wide area — this is a 'community of interest' rather than a strictly local affair. The pool borders Bushey Park and is on royal land, so that royal permission could be 'withdrawn' at any moment, but the park and the pool co-operate over such issues as preventing poachers using the pool as an entrance and exit to the deer-park. Above all Hampton is about community effort both in campaigning to keep a facility alive that local government felt was no longer viable and in sustaining that facility through all manner of fund-raising events, organised since 1993 by the 'Friends of Hampton Pool.' It is also a good example of a 'business-like' solution to a community problem, run as a limited company (with non-remunerated directors) and employing skilled staff for all the specialised tasks associated with running a swimming pool.

The campaign was at its height from 1983 to 1985 under the vivid title of 'Sink or Swim'. Marshall Lees, the guiding spirit and 'team leader' of the campaign group, described to me at a later meeting how he 'ate, drank and slept' the pool for several years. He himself located the campaign as in 'the early years of Thatcherism' — people were beginning to ask interesting and insistent questions about the limits of what individuals could do by 'standing on their own two feet' and what people could do together by renewing the strong vein of associative behaviour in English society. This process both vindicated some of Thatcher's views on the limits of government, and suggested the flaws in her rigid emphasis on individuals and families. In Hampton, there was already an active amenities group (the Hampton Hill Association) and a Residents Association. Marshall himself had been active in local campaigns to share out more equitably the noise pollution of planes arriving and departing Heathrow airport. It also has to be said that the Hampton Pool group were helped considerably by the change of political control on the borough council in late 1983, following a by-election, from Conservative to Liberal. The package eventually put together included GLC funding and a council input, but on the clear understanding that the group itself would run the pool and would have to put up matched funding for the scheme. The support and enthusiasm of local people was overwhelming and the target achieved ahead of schedule.

If Hampton Pool represents the successful face of community action supported by sympathetic politicians, a more recent experience suggests the process may be more complex and contested. This relates to the future use of the old Thames Water filter-beds in Hampton village where a project has been created to establish a village green. Controversy has come over the construction of a cricket pavilion, and Marshall Lees, now a borough councillor himself, has found himself caught between supporters of the council-backed scheme and opponents who fear the pavilion will become a centre for disaffected youth, vandalism and drugs. Marshall described it as 'a bunch of locals fighting us over what we're trying to do for locals', but admitted that they would have to make more effort to involve even more people in the plans if it was to carry the day with public opinion.

In trying to draw general conclusions from the Hampton Pool experience, it is important to recognise the array of talent and contacts the Hampton Pool group was able to assemble in a pleasant, well-heeled London suburb. Not every community will find it so easy to identify and defend its best interest, as I shall show when our journey reaches Oxford and its peripheral housing estates. To deal with the issue here in brief: there are two interrelated and insistent questions in a democracy, albeit coming from rather different political standpoints: who speaks for the powerless in a society, and how can the powerless be given a voice. It has always seemed to me that Morris is ambivalent on this point. As I emphasised in the previous chapter his clear view was that the function of a socialist party is to 'make socialists' and that anything short of that was a waste of time and effort. However, we also saw him softening in his attitude to local government (the London County Council) and it is significant that the softening is related to the willingness of democratically elected councillors to listen to Morris's own pressure group — the Society for the Protection of Ancient Buildings. Thus we can see Morris as in fact part of that long history in England of people coming together with very specific purposes, a history which is quite different from that of political parties, which are characterised as either 'purist' and therefore minority, or 'mass' and therefore always characterised by fudge and compromise.

The history of the Society for the Protection of Ancient Buildings, just as much as that of Hampton Pool, is the history of that other England, of citizen initiative. It is what Shirley Williams at a House of Commons reception for the Council for Education in World Citizenship on 23 March 1998 called 'doing' citizenship rather than just casting your vote. She talked about the gulf between the generations about what constitute public issues, mentioning in particular that while 'drugs' are identified by adults as a public issue, there is widespread abuse of both alcohol and tobacco by those same legislators and would-be legislators. It was curious, given her longstanding differences with Tony Benn (they had been fellow ministers in Wilson's 1960s Labour government) and her status as a life peer in the anachronistic House of Lords, to hear her spelling out the Benn argument that 'traditionally we haven't been citizens, we've been subjects of the Queen'.

This is a quite different view of English history from that of Hampton Court, which is all about kings and famous people whose word is law. But it is of course less than a century from Henry VIII to the trial and execution of Charles I, an event which is quite absent from the account of English history given to the visitor to Hampton Court.

Of history

It pains me to be critical of Hampton Court, as the recipient of their hospitality. Besides, there is so much I love about the place: the range of gardens from the new, fussy, but immature Privy garden; the park with its roe deer; the formal garden with its lawns and clipped yews; the romantic, turn-of-the-century, walled wilderness garden with its massed daffodils and flowering trees over towards the maze, with its literary memories of Virginia Woolf and the much planned, much postponed meeting at Hampton Court in *The Waves*. But it does concern me that in attempting to popularise history, there is always the danger of falsifying by simplification. The aim of the interpretation staff 'to entertain without compromising our reputation as historians' is not an easy one to sustain. And history, in any case, is full of controversy about what events in the past actually 'mean'. For example, our guide told me that she likes to emphasise that in history, 'they do things differently'. She gave the example of Catherine Howard who had to die because her adultery was treason rather than because her husband was an authoritarian, scheming male with a 54-inch waistline and ulcerated sores on his legs. While there is some truth in this, there are also so many aspects of Henry's behaviour which are immediately understandable in the ways men continue to treat women. We saw in the Shakespeare head-quote to this chapter how the subjection of women to men was defended as directly related to the subjection of the subject to the crown. If democracy does not automatically ensure the freedom of every sub-group within society, it still seems to be a necessary pre-condition. At the same time, there is serious discussion of some related issues at Hampton Court. In the afternoon, two costumed women talked of the lives of aristocratic women in Tudor England, their important role as managers of great estates in the frequent absence of their men-folk, and the way in which this role has been ignored by history that sees women merely as wives, mothers and courtesans.

My own tour was described as the 'Tudor' tour, covering as it did the older parts of the palace and the events with which they are most closely connected. As a historian, our guide was both authoritative and informative, recording, for example, the view of William and Mary in the 1690s that Hampton Court was a 'Gothic monstrosity' which should be added to in a more classical and 'European' style. Her style was lively and she moved us at a good pace through the intricacies of the story of Henry VIII. While I confess to having problems about Henry and his wives (I am still stymied by quiz questions which ask you to sort the wives into order and account for their various deaths) I did at least understand the connection with Cardinal Wolsey who had had the palace built and was 'persuaded' by Henry to pass it on to him. I was also able to see that Henry is more in the mediaeval tradition of the peripatetic monarch with palaces in some fifty locations in his realm, rather than the later notion of the monarch in a fixed central palace. In similar fashion, the emphasis placed on the provision of kitchens and apartments at Hampton Court reflected the large numbers of people who constituted Henry's royal 'court'. There is some effort too to move away from a 'Hollywood' view of Tudor life, and our guide was at some pains to take issue with Charles Laughton's portrayal of Henry tearing a chicken apart with his hands and throwing bones to the dog. The relative refinement of Henry's court and the introduction of trends in European thinking and culture into England (for example his collection of two thousand tapestries) through Henry's court are both touched on.

It is not what is said but what is left unsaid which is of real concern. Little mention was made of the central event of mid-sixteenth century England, which is the transition from Catholic England to Protestant England. Above all, this is 'history' from above — a history which although it allows for nuances between the different levels of society involved in court life takes little notice of what is going on outside, beyond the palace walls. Thus, for example, we are told very firmly that sixteenth century children would not have been permitted to sit in the presence of their elders. While this is probably true of the upper echelons of society, it is almost certainly not true of the lower orders, about whose lives, in any case, we have precious little information.

Of heritage

One word that is used a lot at Hampton Court, and indeed throughout what has come to be called 'the heritage indus-

43

try', is 'our'. In general I favour 'our ' (implying what we share with others) especially when contrasted with 'my' (that which I keep to myself and will not share with anyone). However, 'our' can sometimes beg a lot of questions — questions about who 'we' are, of who counts and who doesn't count, about social inclusion and exclusion, about real communities and imagined communities, about real and imagined histories.

Hampton Court is quintessentially English, from Henry VIII to Virginia Woolf. From its hybrid origins in the joining of the Latin and Anglo-Saxons' cultural and linguistic traditions down to the present-day multi-cultural situation, 'Englishness' has been a much-debated concept. If 'Britishness' has now been tossed once and for all beyond the pale, 'Englishness' is not in much better condition as an organising concept for our national identity. In so far as he is concerned with national issues (in the history plays) Shakespeare often takes the easy way out; of asserting national 'English' identity against the other, the foreigner, most often the French. Now Morris is ambivalent about the French. On the one hand he follows that great Victorian artistic and social thinker John Ruskin in identifying the Gothic, and specifically the Gothic of the great northern French churches, as the wellspring of social and artistic health. At other times, the French (and in particular the Norman French aristocracy who became essentially the 'English' ruling class after 1066) are seen as the traditional enemies of English freedoms.

The story, of course, can be taken further back still. There is Alfred, much celebrated in my native county of Somerset, holding the line between 'native' Anglo-Saxons and invading Danes, and creating the conditions for the eventual 'reconquest' of Anglo-Saxon England. The Victorians certainly knew about Alfred, erecting the giant statue to him which dominates the Market Square at Wantage, very close to the middle reaches of the Thames between Reading and Oxford. Take a step further back from Alfred, and there is the myth of Arthur, the myths surrounding Glastonbury and the historical reality of the Celtic people being driven by the Anglo-Saxons into the far west of these islands (Cornwall, Wales, Scotland, Ireland). Myth and history coexist and intertwine: from Alfred's Tower on the Stourhead Estate in Somerset, you can see the pretty little tower on the top of Glastonbury Tor, twenty miles away. The churchyards of Somerset are full of the descendants of Anglo-Saxons, buried under stone Celtic crosses. A step further back, and there are the 'old people' who built Stonehenge and Avebury and littered the Wiltshire and Berkshire downs with their burial mounds. It is an area and a past that William Morris knew well, from his days at school in Marlborough.

We can recognise much more clearly, perhaps, than Morris, that we see in the past what we want to see. We take from the past what we want to take. A modern Morris might well have seen in Gothic not just a special relationship between people and their art, between people and their work, but a unifying principle which suggests a common European homeland stretching from the Atlantic to the borders of Russia; from the Arctic to the Mediterranean. One of the ironies of Hampton Court as 'English heritage' is that it is an intensely European experience. As our guide explains to us, 'England was pretty much a backwater until Henry VIII's time. Henry, if you like, forces England onto the European stage, forces other countries to sit up and take note.' But of course that European dimension to English affairs had been there since Roman times. At the Synod of Whitby, the English church had found decisively in favour of the rites and authority of the Church of Rome over those of the Celtic church. The European Romanesque style comes to us with a European title as Norman. We share equally in the Gothic, and in one sub-style of Gothic (the perpendicular, as in the great 'wool' churches of the Cotswolds and East Anglia, or the chapel at Eton College a few miles down the Thames from Hampton) English Gothic set a standard.

But of course Europe had moved on. From Italy through France into Spain and Germany, the movement we now call the Renaissance was setting other standards, other principles. There is no direct line between the rather quaint and 'mediaeval' buildings of Henry's period at Hampton Court and the severely classical buildings erected alongside at the end of the seventeenth century. Henry may have helped England catch up with the cultural and artistic ideas current in other parts of Europe, but in other ways he does not appear as a good European. His very public divorce from Catherine of Aragon not only soured Anglo-Spanish relations for several centuries but also helped to precipitate the rupture of the Church of England from the authority of Rome.

Morris remains cheerfully oblivious to the contradictory details of national history. His 'turbulent' priest John Ball is a Protestant before his time, with his criticisms of the corruption of the church. But he does not attempt to make the connecting line I shall identify in the next chapter between that concept of freedom as it emerged in medieval England, and the complex set of thinking which emerged on the radical wing of the Protestant movement in the seventeenth century. This democratic thought was a key part in the Civil War and the eventual settlement of the 1689 'Glorious Revolution', which was to make England, in effect, the first parliamentary democracy of modern Europe. Morris cares little for all this. He would probably have found it hard to disguise his boredom at historical research like that of George Rudé and Eric Hobsbawm who carefully plotted the location of the Swing riots in rural 1830s England against the existence of primitive Methodist chapels in the parishes of southern England.[16] Yet Morris does show in general terms how the working-classes that he hoped to win for socialism were the inheri-

---

16. George Rudé and E.J. Hobsbawm, *Captain Swing* (1969, reprinted Pimlico Press, 1993)

tors of popular rights and popular rebellion in defence of those rights, a tradition which is just as much part of 'Englishness' as Henry VIII's strutting and posturing at Hampton Court.

The dynamic between England and Europe does not just exist at the level of 'high art'; of dynastic ambition and international politics, but also at more popular levels. John Ball has his equivalent in any one of a large number of popular 'not quite Protestant but on the way there' movements in late medieval Europe, of which perhaps the long-running campaigns of John Huss and his followers in Bohemia are the best-known. Morris's initiation into politics at the time of the 'Eastern Question' (1876) was prompted by the support of Disraeli's government given to the Turks who were committing atrocities against villages in Bulgaria. Garibaldi in Italy, Victor Hugo in France, Turgenev and Dostoevsky in Russia were others who shared this particular repulsion. The Social Democratic Federation included prominent European exiles such as the Austrian anarchist furniture designer Andreas Scheu. Then there was Eleanor Marx, daughter of Karl Marx, with her 'free marriage' to Edward Aveling. May Morris was later to describe her as 'that gifted and brilliant woman who worked long and valiantly for Socialism.'[17] And always Engels lurking in the background to see that the 'right' political line was taken. There is little doubt in Fiona MacCarthy's mind that Engels guided the schism between Hyndman and Morris which led to the latter's withdrawal from the SDF and the establishment of the Socialist League. On the other hand, MacCarthy is probably equally right in asserting Engels' failure to respond wholeheartedly to 'the imaginative force of Morris, his characteristic and erratic combination of Marxism with visionary libertarianism.'[18]

---

17. MacCarthy, p.508
18. MacCarthy, p.509

Whether we stress the history of popular struggle or the strong European influences on Englishness, clarity is badly needed. Patrick Wright[19] identifies the cult of English heritage and its expression in the English country house as part of the failure of the vision of William Morris and George Lansbury of 'conservation and social reform' and its political expression in the settlement of the Welfare State. What is reasserted, he claims, by modern 'heritage' is something nastier by far. Here he is on the National Trust:

> Established in the 1890s to assert a public interest in landscape and buildings over the delinquency and neglect of private owners, the post-war country house aesthetic now offers to refound the organisation in the French 1790s, aligning it with a reactionary assertion of private meaning, and identifying the public interest with the rampaging egalitarianism of a murderous mob.[20]

I recently examined a recruitment leaflet for the National Trust, of which I am a member. It linked across from the country house, which dominated the buildings illustrated, and controlled landscapes such as those at Stourhead to national emblems such as Winston Churchill and the white cliffs of Dover, with scarcely a mention of its equally important environmental and conservation work.

Maybe Wright exaggerates, or maybe the pendulum has swung once more. The unlamented Department of National Heritage has changed into a more sensible sounding Department of Culture, Media and Sport. I am not sure that what he describes as a 'strain of English socialism, which came down through William Morris to George Lansbury and was finally buried under the deri-

---

19. Patrick Wright, *A journey through ruins: a keyhole portrait of British postwar life and culture* (Flamingo, 1993) p.269
20. Wright, p.97

48

sion of technocratic and Marxist professors in the Sixties'[21] is quite so dead. It is what I would call the 'modest modernity' of the garden city, of interwar public housing estates and health clinics; of the generous instincts of neighbour to help neighbour; the thousand and one kindnesses of everyday life; the associative instinct which keeps our citizens busy with this and that organisation, which make life a little less austere, a little less rawly competitive, than it otherwise would be. Against this 'modest modernity', I will place the uprooting, meta (or mega-?) modernity of the tower blocks, of global capital markets and the arms trade. I shall return briefly to these ideas in the final chapter of the book.

Of nation

To opt for this vision of a modestly modern England is not to seek to build on John Major's woeful 1990s idyll of cricket and warm beer on the village green. The pre-history of this particular view of England as an unpretentious, open society is to be found in Morris's view of England. We have already seen Morris becoming politically active in the Eastern Question Association in 1876; in early 1877 he was a founder member of the Society for the Protection of Ancient Buildings, which aimed not so much to provide protection for neglected buildings, but to protect them from the worst excesses of restorers and rebuilders. At the same time, he was also composing the lecture which he delivered under the title of 'The decorative arts' on 12 April 1877, and which was subsequently published as 'The Lesser Arts' (1878). This is what Morris is so good at; linking art criticism to social criticism, broad brush stuff which begins to hint at the political analysis he was to develop in the 1880s. Morris refers to 'a full sym-

21. Wright, p.269

pathy between the works of man and the land they were made for', before characterising that land as

> a little land; too much shut up within the narrow seas, as it seems, to have much space for swelling into hugeness: there are no great wastes overwhelming in their dreariness, no great solitudes of forests, no terrible untrodden mountain-walls: all is measured, mingled, varied, gliding easily one thing into another: little rivers, little plains, swelling, speedily changing uplands, all beset with handsome orderly trees; little hills, little mountains, netted over with the walls of sheepwalks: all is little; yet not foolish and blank, but serious rather, and abundant of meaning for such as choose to seek it: it is neither prison nor palace, but a decent home.

Yet Morris sees this 'littleness' of England as a source of real, national pride:

> Yet when we think what a small part of the world's history, past, present, and to come, is this land we live in, and how much smaller still in the history of the arts, and yet how our forefathers clung to it, and with what care and pains they adorned it, this unromantic, uneventful-looking land of England, surely by this too our hearts may be touched, and our hopes quickened.

We know that this 'uneventful' land has been the subject of many changes during the twentieth century, some of which are described in this book. Such changes have transformed the appearance of the land, the distribution of population and means of transport. It is interesting to see how over the next decade Morris's own views changed and developed. In his reflective piece in *Commonweal* in 1889, 'Under an elm-tree; or thoughts on the countryside', his reflections are set in a very specific spot, close to the Uffington White Horse which in those days was thought to commemorate Alfred's victory over the Danes at Ashdown in 871 (now generally considered to be of Iron Age origins). Here we can see the direct influence of the Carlyle/Ruskin school of social criticism, of the unequal, brutalising impact of industrialisation on English society:

> Yet I think to myself under the elm-tree, whatever England, once so beautiful, may become, it will be good enough for us if we set no hope before us but the continuance of a population of slaves and slave-holders for the country which we pretend to love, while we use it and our sham love for it as a stalking-horse for robbery of the poor at home and abroad. The worst outward ugliness and vulgarity will be good enough for such sneaks and cowards.

It will be of no use complaining about the 'state of the countryside' or the 'state of the nation' if we have acquiesced meekly in an economy which exalts greed and profit over mutuality and sustainability. In mocking paraphrase of single-minded politicians such as Margaret Thatcher, single-minded in their blind allegiance to the principles of 'the market' and simple-minded in their failure to see any of the personal and social tragedies that the market produces, there is an alternative. Morris's final vision 'under the elm-tree' sums it up:

> Suppose the haymakers were friends working for friends on land which was theirs, as many as were needed, with leisure and hope ahead of them instead of hopeless toil and anxiety, need their useful labour for themselves and their neighbours cripple and disfigure them and knock them out of the shape of men fit to represent the Gods and Heroes? If under such conditions a new Ashdown had to be fought (against capitalist robbers this time) the new White Horse would look down on the home of men as wise as the starlings, in their equality, and so perhaps as happy.

As in *News from Nowhere*, there is the warning that this utopian vision may have to be struggled for. There is no logic of history which will deliver it on a plate. Love of one's nation is not the same as nationalism, which suggests a political system resting exclusively on national identity, or chauvinism ('my country right or wrong'). If we have learned anything from the last century, then it is surely that love of nation is a conditional love. It has to be linked to a readiness to cast a hard look at what a country has become and why; to analyse the source of social issues, and to face up squarely to the de-stabilising force of inequality, based on income but also on gender and ethnicity, in the modern world. A useful analogy is with the true football fan, who knows implicitly that allegiance to a particular team is bound up with a wider love of the game and a willingness also to name problems such as racism and violence on and off the pitch. In a similar way, the true friend of England will know that some issues are above the nation: respect for rights and liberties (which forms the core of the next chapter at Runnymede), respect for different religious and cultural identities within the boundaries of the state, and a willingness to be a good internationalist. Whether England has a future within Britain seems to me increasingly unlikely; it does have a future as a leading member of an enlarged and deepened European Union; it does have a future as a member of international bodies dealing with issues of global stability, the fragile environment of the planet, and the urgent need for a reduction in the proportion of the world's resources which are wasted on weapons of destruction.

The alternative to such a modest 'international' approach to national identity is bleak. The Scots, Welsh and Irish have manifested their desire to go their own separate ways. England within a British shell will rattle horribly and noisily, and risks cracking apart under the kind of pressures which will develop if there is too great a gulf between what we are and what we still pretend to be. Great Britain can affirm its greatness by going quietly — and quickly.

Meanwhile, I look forward to the day when we shall no longer feel the need to be the subjects of anyone. People will still visit Hampton Court and marvel at its beauties, hear stirring stories of past glories, play in the Maze or on the softly flowing Thames. Across the other side of Bushey

Park, the swimmers will carry on swimming, and next door to them, the equally contented allotment holders of Hampton (the site proudly proclaims 'Bushy Park Allotments, 1894-1994') will continue to cultivate their little plots with flowers, fruit and vegetables, and plant their cheerful, rickety huts and sheds in an unplanned way. They are the descendants of the 'free-born English', not the politicians who attempt to lock us into a past which is only bearable because it is exactly that — past and gone for ever.

Chapter 3
Runnymede:
a reflection on democracy

Not in Utopia, subterranean fields,
Or on some secret island, Heaven knows where!
But in the very world, which is the world
Of all of us, the place where in the end
We find our happiness or not at all!
(Wordsworth)

The art of the possible can only be restrained from
engrossing the whole universe if the impossible can find
ways of breaking back into politics, again and again. (E. P.
Thompson)[22]

The Staines line

My visit to Runnymede coincided with the final days of the
long hard winter of Conservative hegemony which began
in 1979. The morning was mild, damp, daffodil- and
forsythia-filled as we trundled down from London on the
train, full of springtime promise as only the south-western
suburbs of London can be on a March morning.
Wordsworth reminds us that happiness is in the 'world of
all of us', the life we lead from day to day, the sum total of
a hundred human kindnesses, a hundred little intimations
of immortality. Utopian thinking, by contrast, places
undue emphasis on the contrast between imperfect present and future perfect. It assumes too that we shall live
to see utopia, a thought that is probably in few people's
minds at present. William Morris in *News from Nowhere* is

---

22. E.P. Thompson, 'Yesterday's Manikin', review of Harold Wilson's
    The Labour Government (1971), reprinted in *Writing by candlelight*
    (Merlin Press, 1980)

keen to emphasise that the change that brought about Utopia was bloody and chaotic. It was a time for heroics but certainly not for happiness. To move from one undesirable state of affairs to another happier one is not a simple matter. The calm life of *Nowhere*, the intoxicating liquor of work and leisure, town and country in equal proportions can only be achieved through bloodshed and suffering. In many ways the world of the twentieth century offered bloodshed and suffering without Utopia. The deal that the advertising at Clapham Junction offers is much simpler. A large hoarding for a financial services firm proclaims the prosaic message that 'Dreams only come true if you budget for them'. Like so much advertising, it seeks to persuade us that only expensive foreign holidays, fast cars and new kitchens arrive bearing the guarantee of happiness.

Like many small towns, Staines has turned its back on the world. At first sight it appears to consist mainly of railway lines, car-parks, a bus-station and a shopping mall. Staines is also the home of that curious television phenomenon, the comedian Ali G, a white Cambridge graduate who makes a living from pretending to be black, Jamaican and semi-literate. This is unfair to Staines. I have simply arrived by the wrong route. The proper route is from the South across Staines bridge from the Surrey side. Hereabouts Surrey and Middlesex do mean something. Staines is now part of the district of Spelthorne running east to the film studios at Shepperton. The meadows of Runnymede, pretty little Egham, the memorials and the Royal Holloway College are all in Surrey. But that is to anticipate. The water-front has both old and new, held together by the already narrowing blue-grey ribbon of the Thames. There are plenty of swans in evidence, despite the fact that local historians and naturalists bemoan the reduction in their numbers. Staines is the second night stop on the annual three-day 'swan-upping' trip from Southwark to Henley, the purpose of which is to mark the Thames cygnets with the same ownership mark as their parents. Ownership is shared between two ancient London guilds, the Company of Vinters or the Company of Dyers, and the Crown, which owns two-thirds of the birds. Nineteen miles from London and between Staines and Runnymede is the London Stone which marked the end of the jurisdiction of the City of London over the River Thames.

Staines suffered at the hands of both parties in the English Civil War, occupied by the Royalists in 1642 and Parliament in 1648. Inevitably the bridge was destroyed. Now all that threatens it is the traffic grinding across its handsome stone arches. There is briefly a cycle track, but this peters out even before you are safely on the north bank, and the continual roar of aircraft taking off and landing at Heathrow Airport, a few miles to the north. Staines puts up with a lot. There is concern for the less fortunate in the community — the old, the sick, those with disabilities or caring for frail relatives. No-one has confidence any longer that 'the state will provide'; a fact for which New Labour ministers must be especially grateful since their leaders no longer seem to regard taxation as a legitimate way of funding essential public services. 'You think it's a rotten world, but there are so many good people in it', the manager of the Volunteer Bureau, himself a volunteer, tells me. People are more isolated now, the old family bonds less secure. I believe him.

A couple of miles along the muddy towpath west of Staines, the M25 motorway, 'the biggest traffic-jam in Europe', rumbles across the Thames, the new concrete bridge sharing the crossing with the older A30 by-pass bridge. Around the Bell Weir lock there is housing on both sides of the river — on the Surrey bank, modest little 1930s mock Tudor bungalows concealed from the towpath by bulky hedges, on the Middlesex shore modern detached houses with picture windows and cabin cruisers moored outside. Just short of Runnymede the towpath opens up into a pleasant park which in turn gives way to the meadows of Runnymede.

The Magna Carta Tea Room

On the narrow greensward between the Staines-Windsor
road and the river, there are early coltsfoot and celandines
in the nervous March sun. Cooper's Hill, north-facing,
steep and well wooded, lies in shadow, with the polished
white stone of the Royal Air Force memorial visible
between the trees on the crest. On the other side of the
road is a broader meadow stretching to the foot of the hill,
with footpaths leading to the 'American' memorials. This
is National Trust property, the whole site having been
donated to the nation in 1931 by Lady Fairhaven. She also
commissioned Luytens, by then an elder of the architectural profession, to design the lodges which now sit either
side of the roadway at the western end of the site. One of
these now bears the legend 'Magna Carta Tea Room',
emblematic of the English ability to turn history into heritage, the sublime into the banal.

Runnymede — the meadow of council — was a traditional meeting place even before Magna Carta. In June
1215, the barons gathered at Staines, while the King was
at Windsor Castle, a few miles to the west. The barons had
had enough of royal demands for money to fight unsuccessful wars in France which were of little interest to
them. What happened at Runnymede was a truce; it marks
merely a stage in the persistent three-way medieval struggle for political power between the church, the crown and
the great land-owners. Yet it has always had enormous
symbolic value. We play fast and loose with our history.
When Margaret Thatcher visited Paris in 1989 for the
bicentenary celebrations of the French revolution, she was
asked whether the French Revolution had any universal
message. Mrs Thatcher replied that she thought not — did
we not have our own Magna Carta? Magna Carta seems to
owe much in retrospect to the emblematic medieval distinction between 'good' and 'bad' government. It is a
notion grounded both in efficiency and ethics. Good government produced peace, good harvests and health. Bad

government produced war, famine and plague. Yet looking back on it we interpret it as a step on the road to democracy. We impose on it our own notion of participation and rights. As Tony Benn said at a televised breakfast picnic at Runnymede more than a decade ago to discuss the nature of democracy, 'If King John and the barons were still here, they wouldn't have understood a word we were saying We'd have been executed as disruptive elements!'[23]

There are elements of Magna Carta which we would recognise as democratic, but there is a limited definition of 'the people'. On the one hand there is the truce between barons and monarch; on the other hand there is an acknowledgement of the rights of another group of growing importance in medieval England — the new urban middle-class of merchants and master craftsmen. It is also important that the notion of 'a freeman' excludes the landless labouring class (the serfs) in the same way as five and a half centuries later the American Bill of Rights was deemed not to apply to slaves. What Magna Carta did do was to lay the foundations for the rule of law:

> No freeman shall be taken, or imprisoned, or diseased (= disturbed), or outlawed, or banished, or anyways destroyed... unless by lawful judgement of his equals or by the law of the land.[24]

Like any statement of rights, it offers a position that can become a rallying point for subsequent attempts to claim or to reclaim their rights by groups of citizens. There is no indication that the nobles interpreted it in any but the

---

23. Tony Benn, personal archives.
24. My account of Magna Carta, the Peasants' Revolt (including quotations from Froissart) and the Putney Debates draws substantially on Jack Lindsay and Edgell Rickword, *A handbook of freedom: a record of English democracy through twelve centuries* (Lawrence and Wishart, 1939). More than one British serviceman carried this in his kitbag during the 1939-45 war as a reminder of why they were fighting. See also Froissart, *Chronicles*, selected, translated and edited by Geoffrey Brereton (Penguin, 1968).

narrowest way, and this is demonstrated by the events that took place in 1381 — usually referred to as the Peasants' Revolt. Women and men of Kent and Essex joined forces in London in an attempt by the 'commons' to appeal directly to the King against what was seen as an abuse of noble power in the imposition of a poll tax. In doing so they were following a strategy which was tried in various parts of Europe in the late middle ages. But in the end, they were thwarted by an alliance between, on the one hand, the 'authorities' of London (the Mayor and the thrusting new middle class) and on the other hand, the nobles and king .

This is how Froissart tells the story in his chronicle:

> When the king heard of their doings he sent his messengers to them, on Tuesday after Trinity Sunday, asking why they were behaving in this fashion, and for what cause they were making insurrection in his land. And they sent back by his messengers the answer that they had risen to deliver him, and to destroy traitors to him and his kingdom. The king sent again to them bidding them cease their doings, in reverence for him, till he could speak with them, and he would make, according to their will, reasonable amendment of all that was ill-done in the realm. And the commons, out of good-feeling to him, sent back word by his messengers that they wished to see him and speak with him at Blackheath. And the king sent again the third time to say that he would come willingly the next day, at the hour of Prime (= 6am or sunrise), to hear their purpose.

It was the barons who subsequently advised the king not to disembark at Blackheath to parley with the rebels.

Described like this, the rebels seem naive and doomed to failure. In any case, it seems likely that far from wanting to shake the foundations of late feudal society, their aims were limited to a strategic attempt to exploit the shortage of labour in the years after the Black Death, in order to secure marginal improvements in their position. That was not how William Morris saw them. He wrote about the

Peasants' Revolt in *A Dream of John Ball* (the work referred to in his *Times* obituary as *A Dream of John Bull!*). It was serialised in *Commonweal* in 1886/87, and the 1892 Kelmscott Press edition contains the famous wood engraving by Edward Burne-Jones: 'When Adam delved and Eve span, Who was then the gentleman', representing a banner described in the book. For Morris, the events of 1381 were a great celebration of fellowship, the making of common cause which is the basis of any political project worth the name. Morris chooses to describe the successes of the revolt and the ideals that inspired it rather than its eventual defeat, while his first person narrator sets up a dialogue with the past that points up the ongoing relevance of this sort of popular struggle in late Victorian England. Yet it is not a naive parallel, but one which reflects the slippery and elusive nature of power:

> "John Ball", said I, "mastership hath many shifts whereby it strives to keep itself alive in the world."

Magna Carta, then, has a symbolic role in the development of English democracy although it may have appeared to be merely a technical adjustment to the knights. There is a small private memorial to Magna Carta, ironically on private land in the grounds of Runnymede House but facing onto the Long Mead. Erected just after the First World War and already partly illegible, the inscription runs: 'Very near to this spot was sealed MAGNA CARTA confirming rights which were in peril and won from King John by the BISHOPS and BARONS for the abiding benefit of the PEOPLE OF ENGLAND and later of the British Dominions and the United States of America.' Bishops, with a few exceptions, and barons, with even less exceptions, have seldom been noted for their contributions to democracy in this country, let alone in the United States of America.

But why no public English memorial? Of course there are practical problems. Members of the Egham Historical

Society told me at their pleasant little museum in Egham that part of the problem was that there is no single spot which could be identified where the signing took place — some people even deny Magna Carta was signed at Runnymede. A Visitors' Centre was planned for the Mead, using the Luytens lodge houses, but turned down by the National Trust. There have been some more recent attempts in Egham by the local Council to turn Magna Carta into local heritage. In the pedestrianised High Street the shields of the barons have been set into the pavement. There is a Magna Carta fountain with water gushing down over the words of the Charter. There is also a considerable statue at the eastern end of the High Street which describes Magna Carta as the 'Great Charter of Democracy'. The unpleasant, box-like little neo-classical parish church adds yet another element to Magna Carta with the inscription above the west door '*Ecclesia anglicana libera sit'* (let the English Church be free).

Another answer is the way that history, especially monumental history, comes to be written by the victors. It still surprises me every time I pass by the Houses of Parliament to see the splendid statue of Oliver Cromwell outside it. But Cromwell did after all have a certain legitimacy as the victor of the Civil War and one of the 'fathers' of English parliamentary government. Further the Commonwealth peters out into just as authoritarian a regime as the royal ones that precede and follow it. In the same Banqueting Hall in Whitehall from where Charles I had stepped out to be beheaded in 1649, both Houses of Parliament met in 1660 to swear allegiance to Charles II. So Magna Carta, with all its symbolic and subversive potential, remains a matter that needs careful handling in a country where we remain 'subjects of the crown' rather than citizens with rights. Perhaps we take democracy for granted: we have a constitution but we do not bother to write it down. Some have argued that the real power of a governing party in the House of Commons has few legal limits. Yet it is wrong, I believe, to talk about Britain as an elective dictatorship. This phrase was particularly used at the time of Margaret Thatcher's long years in office. Yet her rule unravelled in a way that has surprising historical parallels — the Poll Tax with its direct reference back to the complaints of the men and women of Kent in 1381. It was not a constitution that put paid to an arbitrary and unfair tax, but the weight of popular protest. And the power of the people lies in the people's ability to act rather than in any memorial stone. This may go some way to explaining the caution of Tony Blair's first government, as it searches for consensus, despite its very large House of Commons majority.

St George's Hill and the Diggers: 'a common treasury for all'

After 1381, the communitarian ideals that had inspired the Peasants' Revolt went underground to resurface in the libertarian climate of the 1640s. Not far from Runnymede, Egham and Staines is St George's Hill at Weybridge, where a group of radical puritans, inspired by ideals of equality and common ownership, settled on the common land in 1649. Today it is the epitome of the privatised world of the English middle-classes; a large estate of private roads and ugly, pretentious detached houses set among woodland, very similar in feeling to nearby Virginia Water and Wentworth, which in 1999 served as part retreat, part prison, for the Chilean dictator General Pinochet. St George's Hill denies its radical history. Led by Gerard Winstanley, the idealists of 1649 called themselves the Diggers (or True Levellers). They have exercised a powerful influence during the 300 years since the English Revolution, although more recent historical research has suggested that, far from being an isolated occurrence, similar activities to the Diggers' occupation of the commons at St George's Hill were recorded in various parts of England both before and during the Republican period.

There was conscious imitation by the 'The Land is Ours' group which in 1996 occupied the empty Guinness site by the Thames in Battersea, proclaiming that the land should be apportioned according to human needs rather than according to the logic of property-dealing.

The creed of social equality and anti-clericalism is dressed in a special language which the True Levellers inherited from the mediaeval period, not least from John Ball (a priest himself). It is a quasi-allegorical discourse rich in generalities, which condemns all without naming any. Shorn of the specific critique of both feudal and capitalist property relations, it is the language of Blake's Jerusalem too. The description of property as 'sin' goes to the heart of the English Revolution. The same Puritan creed which would later justify the amassing of vast wealth and vast social distance in Victorian England is here used to criticise the very notion of private ownership. 'The world turned upside down', with words and music by Leon Rosselson, expresses the ongoing relevance of the True Levellers to a contemporary social order where inequality has become again the driving principle of enterprise. It is a song which I first heard on a hot summer's night at a children's camp, dedicated to the ideals of co-operation and international solidarity, in the New Forest, and again, a few years later, at a Tolpuddle Martyrs' commemoration rally in the little Dorset village which is so closely linked with the long march of democracy in England.

The world turned upside down
(words and music by Leon Rosselson)

In sixteen forty-nine, to St George's Hill,
A ragged band they called the Diggers came to show the people's will,
They defied the landlords, they defied the laws,
They were the dispossessed reclaiming what was theirs.

We come in peace, they said, to dig and sow,
We come to work the lands in common and to make the waste ground grow,

This earth divided, we will make whole,
So it will be a common treasury for all.

The sin of property we do disdain,
No man has any right to buy and sell the earth for private
gain,
By theft and murder, they took the land,
Now everywhere the walls spring up at their command.

They make the laws to chain us well,
The clergy dazzle us with heaven or they damn us into
hell,
We will not worship the God they serve,
The God of greed who feeds the rich while poor folk
starve.

We work, we eat together, we need no swords,
We will not bow to the masters or pay rent to the lords,
Still we are free, though we are poor,
You Diggers all stand up for glory, stand up now.

From the men of property, the orders came,
They sent the hired men and troopers to wipe out the
Diggers' claim,
Tear down their cottages, destroy their corn,
They were dispersed — but still the vision lingers on:

You poor take courage, you rich take care,
This earth was made a common treasury for everyone to
share,
All things in common, all people one,
We come in peace — the orders came to cut them down.

(Reproduced by kind permission of Leon Rosselson)

The Putney Debates

If the Diggers represent one radical dissenting view in
England's turbulent seventeenth century, the Levellers
represent another. Where the Diggers were inclined
towards direct action, taking themselves off to 'dig and

sow', the Levellers were very much in the thick of the political debates happening in and around the English Civil War. With the royalist army holding the bridge at Kingston and the republicans holding Putney, an uneasy stand-off between the two armies in 1647 created the context for one of the most illuminating of all English political discussions, a discussion which resonates down through the years.

The basic document debated before, during and after the debates in St Mary's Church, Putney in 1647 is usually referred to as The Agreement of the People. As with Magna Carta, there are different versions, and it is not my intention to go into historical detail. The main demands were for equal representation in parliament, 'indifferently proportioned, according to the number of the inhabitants' (i.e. equal constituencies), and parliaments elected for a two year period on a fixed day in March and sitting from April-November. In addition, sovereignty was invested by the people in parliament, and its power was to be 'inferior only to theirs who choose them'. The powers of parliament included enacting laws, erecting offices and courts, appointing and dismissing officers and magistrates, making war and peace, and dealing with foreign states.

Yet parliamentary democracy was not seen as a political system in which people somehow ceded powers to members of parliament. Certain rights were to be retained by the people themselves, especially freedom of religion and the right not to be conscripted into the army. Two critical points were made about the law.

Firstly, there should be equality before the law: 'that no tenure, estate, charter, degree, birth, or place do confer any exemption from the ordinary course of legal proceedings'.

Secondly, 'that as the laws ought to be equal, so they must be good, and not evidently destructive to the safety and well-being of the people', a point which provided a justification for civil disobedience against unjust laws.

Finally, in a categorical statement which still begs many questions, the Agreement of the People claimed: 'these things we declare to be our native rights, and therefore are agreed and resolved to maintain them with our utmost possibilities against all opposition'.

There are a number of issues of current relevance here. For example, there is now widespread support for the idea of fixed term parliaments, to negate the current advantage ruling prime ministers have in being able to fix dates of parliamentary elections (not that it appeared to do more for John Major over the winter of 1996/97 than prolong his agony). There is also the question of rights. The universal Declaration of Human Rights, which underpins much of the work of the United Nations, is a clear statement of the individual rights which national governments should respect. In Britain, this was reflected in growing pressure during the 1990s pressure to integrate the European Declaration of Human Rights into British law. Under the Blair government, this has now happened, and it is now possible to raise cases of violations of human rights within Britain in British courts, rather than having to take them to the European Court. However, the wider question of the possible value of a written constitution remains unresolved.

Much of the debate at Putney centred on the question of the property qualifications for parliamentary elections — a problem not finally resolved until well into the twentieth century. There was a conscious attempt by Ireton and Cromwell, representing the emerging establishment of the Commonwealth, to smear the reputation of the Levellers by association with the communitarian (where not outright communist) views of the True Levellers (Diggers). It was Thomas Rainborough, a representative of moderate Leveller opinion in the New Model Army, who argued for the voice of the propertyless poor to be heard in the affairs of state and for an explicit contract between rulers and ruled:

"...for really I think that the poorest he that is in England hath a life to live as the greatest he; and therefore truly,

66

sir, I think it's clear that every man that is to live under a
government ought first by his own consent to put himself
under that government; and I do think that the poorest
man in England is not at all bound in a strict sense to that
government that he hath not had a voice to put himself
under."

Of course, 'he' and 'man' here mean just that: as Christopher Hill[25] has shown us, it is in the literature of the more
radical of the True Levellers that we must search for any
statement of sexual equality. While there was general
Puritan support for women's rights within marriage —
the right not to be beaten for example — the use of the
term Puritan does suggest an emphasis on both self-con-
trol and social control in sexual relations. Other voices
were heard too, carrying forward the medieval arguments
about women's rights which we hear in Chaucer. In London, both calling a woman a 'whore' and beating one's wife
were outlawed. Milton advocated divorce, while the Quakers were the first to abandon the marriage vow of the
woman to obey the man, on the grounds that both were
equal as they had been in the Garden of Eden. At both
Ranter and Quaker meetings, there were reports of men
and women stripping off their clothes, though as Hill
remarks, it is difficult to know how much of this was exhi-
bitionism and how much was a symbolic expression of
regained innocence.[26]

These arguments about equality between the sexes and
about sexual behaviour are absent from the Putney
Debates. This does not make them unimportant. Ireton
and Cromwell were defending the limitation of the vote to
property owners: Rainborough and the Agitators were
arguing that the distribution of property was in itself
unfair, that it corresponded to conquest (the Norman conquest specifically) and could and should be changed by

25. Christopher Hill, *The world turned upside down* (1972, republished
    Penguin Books, 1975)
26. Hill, p.318

law. They contrasted 'birthright' to 'property right'. It is the logic of this position that two years later took Gerard Winstanley and the Diggers to St George's Hill to lay claim to the land.

It is Rainborough, again, who argues most coherently the need for change, in a way that is surely relevant to our own need for constitutional reform, for a form of government that recognises more explicitly the rights that go with citizenship and brings power closer to the people:

> "I hear it said, 'It's a huge alteration, it's a bringing in of new laws', and that this kingdom has been under this government ever since it was a kingdom.
>
> If writings be true, there hath been many scufflings between the honest men of England and those that have tyrannised over them; and if it be true what I have read, there is none of those just and equitable laws that the people of England are born to, but that they are entrenchments (= intrusions) altogether on the privileges once enjoyed by their rulers. But even if they were those which the people have been always under, if the people find that they are not suitable to freemen as they are, I know no reason to deter me, either in what I must answer before God or the world, from endeavouring by all means to gain anything that might be of more advantage to them than the government under which we live." (Putney 28 October 1647)

It is a pivotal moment in English political history. As a letter writer in the *New Statesman* stated, exploring some of the historical precedents in the communitarian thought of John Macmurray (an important, if indirect, influence on Tony Blair), the key move in Puritanism is the rejection of bishops, and the assertion that authority resides with the congregation:

> Out of the new religions came a new politics via the Long Parliament, the New Model Army, the Levellers, the Diggers, the colonisation of America, the Paineites, the Owenites, the Chartists, the early labour movement ... the emphasis throughout was on belonging, solidarity, reason

and the rejection of arbitrary authority. Blake put it in three words: "Brotherhood is religion".[27]

The Putney Debates, William Morris and the politics of 2000

Substantially rebuilt after fire, St Mary's Putney still stands, close to the Thames, mocking the traffic pouring across Putney Bridge with its legend inscribed on the sundial on the tower: 'Time and tide stay for no man'. It was here in 1647 that the original Putney Debates took place. Here in the 1980s, Labour politicians such as Tony Benn and Peter Hain (candidate for Putney in 1983 and 1987) debated the way forward for a party which appeared to have lost not only the battle for people's votes, but any sense of a future at all. And here in 1997 the Quakers organised a weekend celebration for the 350th anniversary of the original debates, at which a new agreement of the people, a new agenda of environmentalism, people-oriented economics and North-South solidarity was debated.

The case for the Levellers is an easy one to make — representative government, equal rights, and all that that implies, even if there are aspects of that agenda still to be fully implemented. More difficult is the case against them. Yet the Cromwell/Ireton position is important because it makes the point that the ownership of property is considered in our democratic but capitalist societies to be a fundamental right. That is one problem. Another is what we know about how democratic ideals have been perverted in the name of an authoritarianism of the Left which is the mirror-image of that of the Right. As Milan Kundera, a Czech novelist with direct experience of such tyranny, puts it in his novel *The Unbearable Lightness of Being*, do we really want to march to the tune of any mob?[28] Kun-

27. Peter Cadogan, *New Statesman*, 14 February 1997, p.36
28. Milan Kundera, *The unbearable lightness of being* (Faber, 1984)

dera is making the point that it is precisely this uniformity which threatens individual freedom and liberty as much as private ownership of property and the means of production, and control of information flows. While the Levellers and Diggers have been feted by subsequent generations inspired by various forms of socialist thought, there was much in seventeenth century Puritan thought that was narrow and depressing, when not actually obscurantist and bizarre.

Morris, curiously, would have agreed. As I argued in the opening chapter, Morris takes from Marx the notion of violent upheaval as the way of producing change in society — indeed this is the central and justifying sequence of *News from Nowhere*, the events which change dystopia into utopia. But the outcome is a Utopia very different from anything that has ever been produced by socialist revolution. There is a certain level of social discipline, which I would call simply a recognition of obligation to other people, but very little overt control. An emphasis on the rights of property is replaced by a generalised sense of joy in, and generosity towards, other people. The citizens of *Nowhere* behave as if surrounded by a secret garment of freedom which informs their work, their relationships with one another and with their environment. I fancy that neither seventeenth century Puritan ministers nor hardline twentieth century Communist Party members would have approved. Without using religious language, it is as if Morris has taken from the thought of the seventeenth century precisely that idea of a divinely inspired inner conscience which is so characteristic of the radical Leveller thought that Christopher Hill spent so much of his working life exploring.

There are other themes that Morris would have recognised. For example, Fiona MacCarthy, in her recent biography of William Morris, points out the remarkable element of sexual politics in *A Dream of John Ball*, in which strong men weep and women are partners in the political endeavour: 'the narrative shimmers with half-hints and provocations'.[29] Certainly the theme of the common ownership of land and property for benefit of all is central to much of Morris's writings. There is also the Garden of Eden argument about individual and collective responsibility to preserve the diversity and fecundity of nature, which is very apparent in the way the Diggers wrote about the stewardship of the land, and is again apparent in Morris. Finally there is the same tension between the exponents of the inner light which guides human action towards good, and the more prosaic assumption, apparent in the Putney debates, that people must be led towards the good by wisely formulated constitutions and laws. It is to the question of law that we now turn.

A little bit of America: the presence of the USA at Runnymede

It is possible to glide through Runnymede, eyes fixed on the sparkling Thames, to have a cup of tea at the Magna Carta tea-room and continue on to Royal Windsor without regard to the strong presence on the hillside of another group of unruly rebels against royal authority: the colonies which were eventually to become the United States of America.

To the left is the elegant little pavilion erected by the American Bar Association in 1957, with its column of Cornish granite inscribed 'To commemorate Magna Carta, symbol of freedom under law'. It is a curious interpretation of Magna Carta. There is of course a sense in which freedom is indeed protected by law. It is the sense we give to freedom when we talk about freedom of thought or freedom of the press. But there are also real senses in which the law has always limited people's freedom, whether in the name of powerful interest groups, private property or

29. MacCarthy, p.548

71

social well-being. The memorial also records, more broadly, that on subsequent visits by the American Bar Association they pledged their adherence to the 'principles of the Great Charter', which would seem to go rather further than the original inscription.

As with most heritage sights, we are not simply left to make up our own minds. The National Trust has 'helpfully' provided a guide to the memorial which explains that 'Freedom under the law' was not only a principle of Magna Carta but went on to form the basis of the United States constitution and Bill of Rights, 'of which Thomas Jefferson said: "All men are created equal in life, liberty and the pursuit of happiness".' Now this is heady stuff indeed to contemplate as the jumbo jets climb steeply from Heathrow and bank south across Runnymede, perhaps carrying another group of heritage-loving Americans back home. It is well known that Jefferson managed to square his views on democracy with his status as the owner of a Southern plantation dependent on slave labour. The contradictions of his position rumbled on into the nineteenth century. In general terms the Bill of Rights was deemed not to apply to slaves and indigenous people. While the Civil War dealt with the issue of slavery, the question of Civil Rights for black people remained to be fought out in the second half of the twentieth century, while indigenous Americans lost their lands and their freedoms to the white settlers as the United States advanced across the Mid West towards the Pacific.

There was no legal basis for the revolt of the colonies, any more than there was for anti-imperialist struggles in modern Africa and Asia. Such struggles depend ultimately on a more general view of 'right' and 'wrong', and a tradition of natural justice resonating down through the centuries. When Morris writes of the 'injustice' of nineteenth century England, he is writing of the hundred and one ways in which inequality was actually written into the laws of the land. It is a position much closer to Rousseau and the view that 'man is born free, but is everywhere in chains.' The right to oppose unjust laws, to enact new laws and to modify existing ones is just as fundamental a democratic right as the notion of the 'rule of law'. That was exactly the point Rainborough made in Putney church on the 28th October 1647, or at least that is how we read Rainborough today.

There is of course a separate question around establishing and maintaining rights. Rights can also be conservative arguments, as the debate on property rights at Putney in 1647 shows. In the USA, one of the most violent societies in the world, the right to carry guns is referred right back to the Constitution itself, and is backed by a powerful lobbying group. In the United Kingdom, a fundamental right which has never been established is the right of people to be citizens in a constitutional democracy rather than subjects of the Queen. The 1689 English Bill of Rights refers to the rights of parliament rather than the rights of the people, and has been infamously abused in recent years to avoid proper public scrutiny of the dealings of Members of Parliament, as in the 1990s 'cash for questions' scandal. But even supposing there were a set of rights established as part of a new constitutional settlement, the question of maintaining and interpreting rights remains a central political concern. Just as black people and women have had to struggle hard and long to establish that they too are covered by the concept of rights, so people with disabilities have only begun the struggle to establish their rights as equal to those of the rest of humanity. If political rights are the starting-point, the end-point must surely be a concern for the economic and social rights of citizens. If 'freedom under the law' is a starting-point, 'justice under the law' is the desirable end-point.

All this has a powerful resonance in William Morris. Although his attack on the political basis of nineteenth century capitalism was a relative failure, his attack on the moral basis of nineteenth century capitalism still makes compulsive reading. Here is Morris writing in *How I became a Socialist* (1894):

Apart from the desire to produce beautiful things, the leading passion of my life has been and is hatred of modern civilization... What shall I say concerning its mastery of and its waste of mechanical power, its commonwealth so poor, its enemies of the commonwealth so rich, its stupendous organization — for the misery of life! Its contempt of simple pleasures which everyone could enjoy but for its folly? Its eyeless vulgarity which has destroyed art, the one certain solace of labour?

And, on the other hand, the virtues of socialism (from *How we live and how we might live*, written in 1884):

Well, now, what Socialism offers you... is, once more, regulation of the markets; supply and demand commensurate; no gambling, and consequently (once more) no waste; not overwork and weariness for the worker one month, and the next no work and terror of starvation, but steady work and plenty of leisure every month; not cheap market wares, that is to say, adulterated wares, with scarcely any good in them, mere scaffold-poles for building up profits; no labour would be spent on such things as these, which people would cease to want when they ceased to be slaves. Not these, but such goods as best fulfilled the real uses of the consumers would labour be set to make; for, profit being abolished, people could have what they wanted instead of what the profit-grinders at home and abroad forced them to take.

If the American Bar Association memorial is modest and thought-provoking, the John F. Kennedy memorial, a hundred yards along the hillside, is more like a bad Hollywood epic. Yet it begins well. You cross the stile onto a small plot of American soil. For a moment, climbing the steps through the English woodland, the bird song silences the drone of traffic and the jets throwing themselves into the afternoon sky. The path climbs steeply, twisting gently, not revealing the memorial until the last moment. A simple stone, with a lovely view across the spring-bright greensward. My problems began on reading the inscription, taken from Kennedy's 1961 Inaugural Address:

> We shall pay any price, bear any burden, meet any hardship, support any friend or oppose any foe in order to assure the survival and success of liberty.

Well, yes, but... McCarthyism? Vietnam? Central America? the CIA? The fearful years of the Cold War when people's very existence seemed to hang like a thread between the White House and the Kremlin?

Worse was to follow with the twin seats and their respective paths set to the side of the memorial. On an earlier visit I had paid little attention to this; on this occasion I had time to return to the National Trust heritage plaque at the foot of the path, to 'discover' that these paths are symbolic of the president and his consort, the King and Queen, or indeed of man and woman in general. Needless to say, one is set symbolically lower than the other. The pleasant pathway up through the woods turns out to be symbolic of the relationship between individual and society: 60,000 axe-hewn Portuguese granite setts laid at random. I quote: 'the craftsmen were unable to comprehend this need for individuality, and could only complete their task when the steps were likened to the uneven appearance of a crowd at a football match.' One wonders as ever whether to blame the workers or their managers. Poor Morris would surely have managed a quiet chuckle, although his views on the 'beautiful game' have not, to my knowledge, ever been recorded.

...And finally — 'The wood symbolises the virility and mystery of nature as a life force and it reflects beautifully the scenario of life, death and spirit as the wood changes naturally throughout the seasons.' Possibly. John F. Kennedy was not a saint, and does not deserve to be treated as one. Perhaps we need something more modest by which to remember great leaders, something which represents the common humanity we share, and the conditional relationship of people and rulers in a mature democracy.

An enabling politics

Democracy is something we fight for, work for, something enacted (or otherwise) in our daily lives. Government is a necessary evil, as Tom Paine wrote in *Common Sense* in 1776:

> Government, even in its best state, is but a necessary evil; in its worst state, an intolerable one. Government, like dress, is the badge of lost innocence; the palaces of kings are built upon the ruins of the bowers of paradise.

But how to regain paradise? For me, the business of government is to ensure the conditions under which democratic rule, and self-rule, can flourish at the most local level possible, down to and including each individual. We inhabit a limited democracy in which the sense of empowerment, of being in control of our own individual lives and the lives of the communities in which we live, is not a common experience. Perhaps it is the result of too many years of monopoly of power by a single party. Perhaps, too, 1997 may have been the dawn of something better and bolder. But many, many people feel powerless to change anything. Even more worrying, they no longer believe in the possibility of change. Morris, of course, despised the 'game' of parliamentary politics. For him, the only task was to 'build socialists'. For us, it is perhaps a more basic task of building people who can dare to hope that the future may not only be different but better than the present.

At times, that hope may lead us into bitter conflict with others, as it did in the armed struggle against fascism in World War II. The one memorial at Runnymede which I have yet to mention is the RAF memorial, perched on the top of Cooper's Hill. It commemorates twenty thousand, four hundred and fifty-five people who gave their lives in wartime and have no known grave, with the simple inscription 'They died for freedom'. This stark memorial with its profound silence and oppressive solemnity is a sobering but also an inspiring place. Even the Queen managed to strike the right note here, referring in her address at the opening in 1953 to Runnymede and the 'seed of liberty which helped to spread across the earth the conviction that man should be free and not enslaved.' As Morris writes in the final lines of *News from Nowhere*:

> Go on living while you may, striving, with whatsoever pain and labour needs must be, to build up little by little the new day of fellowship, and rest, and happiness.
>   Yes, surely! and if others can see it as I have seen it, then it may be called a vision rather than a dream.

In social terms, optimism remains the most rational of all philosophical positions, because without it the future will be as dark as our darkest fears.[30]

---

30. See also John Payne, 'William Morris: back to the land, pessimism and utopia', *Journal of the William Morris Society*, Spring 2000.

Chapter 4
Windsor, Eton and Slough

I am sick of ministering to the swinish luxury of the rich.
(William Morris)

England! awake! awake! awake!
Jerusalem thy sister calls!
Why wilt thou sleep the sleep of death,
And close her from thy ancient walls? (William Blake)

Even the length of rivers, it seems, is uncertain in our age of doubt and relativism. The Aerofilms Guide to the Thames Path offers two hundred and thirteen miles on page four, but two hundred and fifteen on page eight, both lengths carefully translated into their different metric equivalents.[31] The Thames is generally recognised to rise at a spring beneath an ash-tree in a Cotswold meadow called Trewbury Mead, although the same guide admits that for its first two miles the great river is 'merely a winding, grassy hollow'. Perhaps it is these first two miles that are discounted in the preface... Most people walk the Path, an officially recognised long-distance path like the Pennine Way or South-Western Coastal Path, from source to sea, the moment of its arrival being defined by the Thames Barrier. For Joan and Georgiana from Westbury in Wiltshire (but originating respectively from Southwark and the East End) it was a two summers' enterprise, walking at the steady pace of ten miles per day and staying overnight in bed-and-breakfasts along the route. I met them at Runnymede, a good place to meet anyone, I thought. They are members of the Ramblers' Association and do voluntary work to keep themselves busy. They are the sort of older people whose age you carefully avoid asking about, unless they volunteer the information.

---

31. Helen Livingstone, *The Thames path* (Ian Allan Publishing, no date)

They said 'You meet a lot of people out walking', and I think this was certainly true for them. At four miles an hour, or even three, which is enough for me, you don't meet so many, because you have to keep the rhythm going. But at ten miles a day there is time to stop and chew the cud occasionally.

From Runnymede to Windsor, walking in the opposite direction to that taken by the Westbury Londoners, the Path is not so easy either. The road hugs the river closely at first, and the towpath walker is reduced to the indignity of pavement walker. It is very easy without a guide to pass through Old Windsor without noticing that this particular bit of roadside suburban sprawl was once the seat of kings in Saxon times. It was only as recently (in an old country like England) as 1110 that Henry I moved the court to his new palace at present-day Windsor. Beyond Old Windsor the river indulges in a quite excessive meander which was by-passed by a cut and lock in 1822. Only a few steps beyond this, the Path makes a dramatic detour of its own, across the Albert Bridge to Datchet and then back via the Victoria Bridge into Windsor itself, with one aim in mind — to avoid the private royal grounds of Windsor. The bridges themselves were built in 1851 to replace the river crossing at Datchet village, for reasons which we shall see below.

It is a symbolic moment. Hampton Court is merely the pretence of royal power, the monarchy having long discarded it to grace and favour residents, tourists and children. Windsor Castle is the real thing, a one hundred and ten percent symbol of continuing authority. Badly damaged by fire a few years ago, it has been rebuilt at enormous expense. It is a useful reminder that, if we are to seek out the 'swinish rich' in modern Britain, the search begins with the Royal Family. Despite Queen Victoria donating Windsor Great Park to the nation in 1851 after the Great Exhibition, the Home Park remains in royal hands. The result of this is that much of this stretch of the river has no towpath, with the houses and gardens of Datchet on one bank and the Home Park on the other. The boat commentary on my return from Windsor by river launch later in the day, refers to 'security' reasons for keeping the public out of this particular piece of land! Perhaps in the wake of revelations about the efforts of MI5 in phone-tapping and keeping files on a number of cabinet ministers in the Labour government, including Jack Straw, the Home Secretary, it is time to stop using security as shorthand for privilege. Fortunately it is not a state secret that the river crossing at Datchet village was removed on the instructions of Queen Victoria who didn't like the peasants 'in her back garden'. For good measure, she had an Act of Parliament passed to enclose the Home Park. Thus one Englishwoman, at least, at the end of the twentieth century could still describe her home as her castle.

It is a pretty view though. After a hot but wet summer there is much luxuriant growth and second flowerings along the riverbank. At Old Windsor Lock the giant sunflowers hang over the water like trees, the elderberries drip in bunches from the trees and there are plump ripe blackberries too. At Datchet a forest of maize has sprung up between the river and the castle. When I eventually caught up with the film 'Robinson in Space' on television, I discovered that Robinson, or rather the film's director Patrick Keiller, had also passed this way. There is a lingering shot across the wall at the Albert bridge with CROWN ESTATE — PRIVATE GROUNDS inscribed in bold capital letters, lest the high pointed railings and castellated gate house are insufficient message for the passer-by. It is all a question of which angle one decides to look from; what is in focus and out of focus.

On the boat back many of the passengers are talking about Princess Diana, buried on an island on another private estate only the previous Saturday. They tell me that Windsor Castle is 'full of lovely flowers for Diana'. I have just come back from a rain-sodden walking holiday in Scotland and feel baffled by it all. Is it a 'defining moment' or an outbreak of mass hysteria? Are we as a nation ready to turn our backs if not on the monarchy, then on a particular conception of the monarchy as privilege? Or is Diana simply a victim of the need we so often feel to transfer our hopes, fears and desires onto one person, who always turns out to be imperfect, as we ourselves are? Perhaps the most interesting feature has been the young Prime Minister, Tony Blair, advising the elderly Queen on what to do, what to say, how to present the royal family to the nation. Perhaps no royal decision has ever been greeted with such popular outrage as her decision not to fly the flag at Buckingham Palace at half-mast to mark the passing of the folk-heroine princess. Having dragged the Labour Party into the modern world, was Blair now about to do the same for the monarchy? But in any case this would suggest a trimming of the symbolic and economic power of the monarchy to match the trimming of its political power.

A year, two years on, much of this seems like journalistic froth on the dark and murky waters of the English establishment. Yet that picture of the unmistakable profile of Windsor Castle rising serenely above the trees, the quiet meadows in the middle distance and the forbidding foreground of walls and railings, remains. The symbolic power of the monarchy comes from its position at the apex of the class structure and ownership of wealth. This is the point that cannot be evaded or turned into journalism. Raymond Williams, in *The Long Revolution*,[32] attempted to find a continuity in English cultural history, a slow unwinding in the direction of greater democracy, greater equality. Yet in many ways the Thatcher years reversed that movement. There is greater inequality than previously, the powers of local government, as against those of the central state, have been eroded. There is little indication as yet that the Labour government has any intention of reversing either of these processes. In their public statements they adhere to the same language of the trickle-

---

32. Raymond Williams, *The long revolution* (Chatto and Windus, 1961)

down theory which we have heard so often from Conservative politicians: if the economy grows, then increased wealth will be shared out all the way down to the bottom of society.

The bottom of society seems an awfully long way down. We are no longer talking of a trickle down to a united and well-organised working class. The working class, as we shall see in Oxford in chapter eight, has become fractured and disorganised, partly by the weakness and decadence of its own organisational structures, partly by the deliberate action of government. Yet the persistence of class as a way of thinking about English society and, more importantly, of placing oneself in relation to others, is one of the most remarkable features of modern England. For example, between 1964 and 1996, the proportion of people acknowledging the existence of a class struggle increased from one half to three quarters.[33] This is even more surprising bearing in mind that the survey question attempted to place class struggle in the past: "There used to be a lot of talk about a 'class struggle'. Do you think there is a class struggle in this country or not?"

Below any lingering identity of 'working people', there are the millions whose livelihood now depends on state benefits of one kind or another. Again, this has not been an accidental process, with at least three identifiable broad trends resulting from government policy in the 80s and 90s. Firstly there was the failure to implement minimum wage regulations, so that low wage employers were in effect subsidised by the payment of benefits such as Family Credit to those on low wages. There is, of course, minimum wage legislation now in place, but there is still concern over the low level at which the minimum has been set, and the lack of mechanisms for its enforcement. Secondly, the failure to act on historically very high levels of

---

33. Brian Deer, 'Still struggling after all these years', *New Statesman*, 23 August 1996 (Source: Gallup Organisation)

unemployment through the 80s and early 90s. Although this level was falling by the end of the century, it is still sufficiently high to mean that people have little alternative but to accept the many low-paid, part-time and temporary jobs on offer. And thirdly the creation of mass poverty among older people dependent on the state pension by the severing of the link between pensions and average wages. In many ways this last point sums up the moral bankruptcy of the Conservative governments from 1979-98. Here was a generation which had fought and won the war against Hitler and fascism, which had fought and won the struggle for the National Health Service and the Welfare State. The image of a pensioner couple struggling to keep warm in winter but frightened about how to pay the bills if they turn the heating on or up must be placed alongside the image of Joan and Georgiana on a golden autumn day at Runnymede. Yet despite Christmas bonuses and warm words, it is another challenge that has not been met by the Labour government.

Of Windsor I will say little more... There is after all plenty and enough in the standard tourist literature. Windsor is dominated by all the outgrowths of international tourism, with McDonald's, the despoilers of so much good quality, subsistence farming land in Central America, in a key location on the way up to the castle. With Stratford, Windsor seems to be one of only two compulsory tourist venues in England outside London. It is all very odd. Yet the Official Guide to the palace does manage to reflect the debate about the future of the Royal Family, albeit unintentionally. The obsequious and openly imperialist ending to the historical introduction is predictable:

> One of the most notable buildings in our national heritage, it is visited by many thousands of people every year. From it the Royal Family takes its name, and to it the eyes of British people the world over turn in affection and loyalty.

I cannot speak for Britain, let alone for 'British people the world over', but there are rather less predictable words here which perhaps reflect the way many people in England have come to feel about their extremely enlarged and extremely expensive royal family. This is the description of the foundation of Windsor Castle:

> Here in about 1070 King William erected, or rather caused his new and reluctant subjects to erect, an unusual example of the "motte and bailey" castle.

Subjects, yes; reluctant, yes. But no longer new, since many of us have now been subjects of Queen Elizabeth II for nearly 50 years.

There is also the question of whose queen she really is. Most of the other boat passengers returning from Windsor to Runnymede are two coachloads of elders — one white, the other Asian. It is not enough, it seems, for we English to be subjects of the queen, but millions of other people across the world are bound into the same position by the largely meaningless institution of the Commonwealth. I recall my closest encounter with royalty — a seminar at St James's Palace organised by an international aid agency. It was strange enough to be discussing international poverty in the plush gilded cage of a royal palace. Stranger still was the instruction to the participants that when His Royal Highness, Prince Charles, entered the room, we were all to stand and remain standing until he sat down. Those complying with this bizarre request included democratically elected ministers from several African and Asian nations.

However, for the thousands of Asians who live just across the river from Windsor, in its twin town of Slough, the most apparent problems are little to do with being subjects of the Queen, and much more to do with jobs, and education, and housing. It is easy to see why Morris, in focussing on the inequality, poverty and waste generated by capitalism, remained silent on the already largely redundant institution of Queen Victoria and her family. Like the state in classic Marxist theory, it was no doubt intended to wither away. Like the state itself it remains as the symbolic tip of the iceberg of privilege and inequality.

Writing in the *New Statesman* in 1998,[34] Paul Barker's only mention of the large Asian population in Slough is the throw-away comment that 'Cleaners — often Asian — trek from here into Heathrow.' Having already written an article in the *Independent* about Slough (17 February 1990), one feels Barker could have done better. My own conversations in Slough suggested that race-blindness is not uncommon here. For example, I was surprised to be told by several people in Slough that the 1991 census figure of 25% Asians overstates the true figure. Yet because so many Asians are young, providing about a third of the school population of the town, the figure is set to grow. In addition to Asians, Slough also has smaller African and Afro-Caribbean minorities, so that white children are only one half of the school population. The prospects for many of these children are not good, in communities where unemployment is still a problem. Thus while many in the Thames valley oppose the plans for a fifth terminal at London airport, many in Slough support it, because it will bring more jobs to the area.

My own personal memories of Slough are not untypical; a series of well regulated traffic lights while hitch-hiking on the A4 between my home town of Bath and London in the 1960s. I managed to miss Betjeman's onslaught on Slough, indeed more or less anything and everything about Slough, until I read Patrick Wright's book *A Journey through Ruins*. This led me back to Betjeman's lines

Come, friendly bombs, and fall on Slough.
It isn't fit for humans now.

34. Paul Barker, 'Observations', *New Statesman*, 27 March 1998, p.62

If Betjeman was attacking the randomness of Slough, its lack of urban pattern and organisation, its preference for 'housing' over architect-designed houses, in a word its 'American' quality, Wright takes this further by linking it up with Prince Charles's espousal of traditional architectural values, as in his Mansion House speech in 1987:

> "You have, Ladies and Gentlemen, to give this much to the Luftwaffe: when it knocked down our buildings, it didn't replace them with anything more offensive than rubble. We did that..."[35]

It is popular to be harsh on Charles. Snob, stick-in-the-mud, emotionally underdeveloped he certainly is. Yet his concern for the environment is a real one, and through the Prince's Youth Business Trust he has enabled a committed staff to promote ideas of enterprise and economic independence among young people during a difficult period when the economy has simply not been producing many jobs for them.

Wright's overall point is that Charles is part of a process whereby repeated attempts to turn England into a modern, dynamic country have foundered on establishment views. These are often reflected and supported in the popular press, which emphasises England-Britain as a 'heritage country' tied by visual symbols into the past. He concludes:

> This is the fundamental problem at the centre of Charles's 'Vision of Britain'. The revivalist fable articulates truly vital cultural themes, but it submits them to a morbid process of simplification, which can itself come to stand in the way of proper understanding... there is something scandalous as well as trivializing about the way in which an argument about architectural style has been used to obliterate the fact that, for many people at the time, the post-war reconstruction was the memorial:

---

35. In Wright, *A journey through ruins*, p.360

there was to be a 'New Britain', not just a fancy obelisk in the ground.[36]

That post-war construction included the right to well-built homes, a National Health Service and a Welfare State to protect the very young and very old and the rest of the population at times of social pressure such as unemployment or starting a family. Social reality cannot be reduced to cultural icons, which may help to explain why Morris designs are so often the badge of snobbery and social exclusiveness rather than of the democratic values he preached to the London working-class.

Is it too crude a contrast, that between the English standing joke of Slough, the town you never know you've been to until you see the sign saying you're leaving it, Windsor, the profile of its castle one of the few silhouettes which most English people would recognise at once, and Eton, the traditional home of English snobbery and class difference? Maybe, but it is a curious accident of place which finds them located so conveniently near to one another. Slough may have its problems, but is Windsor any better? How does it help the schools in Slough to know that Prince Charles's sons have mixed with 'ordinary' boys by attending Eton College rather than completing their education with private tutors, as used to be the habit with members of the royal family? Unsurprisingly, in the unitary authority break-up of the old county of Berkshire, both Windsor and Eton have found themselves linked into middle-class Maidenhead rather than working-class Slough.

Capitalism stands naked in the face of ethical interrogation, guilty as charged of promoting greed, brutal competition, massive structured inequalities and the use of force to crush dissent. And this is where we turn to Morris. Although the precise context of these times is so different from the 1890s, what seems truer by the year is his portrayal of the ethical hole at capitalism's heart. Much of Morris follows

---

36. Wright, p.365

Marx closely, and there are serious problems about reading off Marxist analysis onto the modern world. But the ethical argument still stands as Morris wrote it. In this light, it is Windsor, rather than Slough, which is the problem town. Yet the macro-problems of Windsor — unreasonable wealth, inequality, subservience — must not blind us to the everyday micro-problems of Slough — the personal experience of unemployment, racial tension and insufficiently funded public services. Both need working at.

Slough grew in the 1930s with the influx of large numbers of unemployed Welsh men and women heading up the Great Western Railway, following the coal trains that took Welsh coal to the fires and furnaces of the London area. It was a pre-eminently capitalist organisation, the Slough Estates, which provided much of the impetus to the growth of consumer factories in the Slough area, such that the town grew from only just over ten thousand people in 1900 to thirty-three thousand six hundred and twelve at the 1931 census, sixty-six thousand four hundred and seventy-one in 1951 and around one hundred thousand at the end of the century. Slough acted as a gateway into British Empire markets for European firms in the 1920s and '30s, just as more recently American and Asian firms have used Britain with its low wage rates and cowed trade unions as a bridgehead into the European Union marketplace.

Conditions in Slough were often dire. The Welsh workers were housed in timber huts on concrete sleepers. When the inhabitants dared to criticise this 'Timbertown', the local Tory MP, Sir Alfred Knox, who had commanded a White Russian brigade against the Bolsheviks at the end of the First World War, stated:

> 'There used to be some wooden huts at Aldershot barracks which were built at the time of the Crimean War. I found them quite comfortable to live in.'[37]

---

37. In Michael Cassell, *Long lease! The story of Slough Estates* (Pencorp Books, 1991)

More recently the Slough Estates company has been one of the more reputable financial supporters of the Tory Party. More controversially, it has also supported the right-wing free market organisation Aims of Industry which is among the noisiest advocates of restricting trade union rights. This opposition to trade union activity is on the grounds that the collective organisation of workers prevents the market from working as it was intended to. Needless to say, it is not clear, of course, whose intentions are referred to.

Like so many towns, though, Slough is more and more about buying and selling than about making things. It is ironical that one of the icons of this shift is the large Co-op store at the junction of the A4 from London and A412 from Watford. It is not clear to me exactly whether the 'real uses of consumers', to use Morris's terms, are being attended to here. Are the shoppers in the Co-op simply buying what the producers have determined they shall buy? Is there nothing of value here? Even if one looks at supermarkets as purveyors of foodstuffs polluted by insecticides and pesticides, this is balanced by the fact that they are now a major outlet for organic vegetables and fruit.

Large supermarkets, co-operative or otherwise, reflect many of the contradictions of our society in most imaginable ways. Not only are the workers of Slough better housed, but they are also better fed and clothed than the workers of the 1890s. Capitalism depends on their consumption more than it does on the consumption patterns of the 'idle rich.' It is the same argument we saw in chapter one in Walthamstow and Merton. It will not do to dismiss today's shoppers as mere dupes of capitalism. Amid the vulgar and the second-rate, people are making choices that have meaning for them about how they wish to live. What may be of more concern are the cartels operated by large supermarkets and other retail chains which, in order to keep profits high, charge much higher prices for fresh food, electrical goods and cars than is the case in the rest of Europe or in the United States of America. In addition, many small towns in England have suffered extensively in recent years from the building of supermarkets and other large-scale retail outlets in out-of-town locations. Not only is it necessary to use a car to reach them, but smaller businesses left behind in the town centres often find it difficult to survive without the trade drawn in by the larger stores. Even if we accept that large supermarkets are here to stay, there are still decisions to be made.

Morris defines the moral problem, even though his particular political positions did not lead to positive outcomes. And his positions on both capitalism and socialism need to be redefined for a more complex world than the one he knew. Perhaps Edmund Wilson, writing sixty years ago in his classic study *To the Finland Station*, summed it up best:

> When all this is said, however, something important remains that is common to all the great Marxists: the desire to get rid of class privilege based on birth and on difference of income; the will to establish a society in which the superior development of some is not paid for by the exploitation ... of others — a society which will be homogenous and co-operative as our commercial society is not, and directed, to the best of their ability, by the conscious creative minds of its members. But this again is a goal to be worked for in the light of one's own imagination and with the help of one's own common-sense.[38]

'Class privilege based on birth and difference of income' remains a major feature of English society. A key mechanism in achieving and sustaining this has been our education system. The state system of education from William Forster's Education Act of 1870 onwards has always been ambitious — ambitious to set up a system to rival that of the private schools which were organised in Victorian England. Of course many of these schools were based on late mediaeval foundations which had aimed to provide a

---

38. Edmund Wilson, *To the Finland station: a study in the writing and acting of history* (1972, reprinted Penguin, 1991)

charitable education for boys of the lower orders in society who wished to become priests. Hence the very quaint use of the term 'public' to describe such schools. Yet despite the tripartite system set up following the 1944 Education Act, with its grammar, technical and 'modern' schools, despite the move to the single 'comprehensive' secondary school, despite the raising of the school leaving age to 15 and then to 16, the English education remains characterised by elitism.

For every effort to impose greater equality there is an equal, and sometimes greater, reaction to assert difference, distinction, nuances. Recent experience in higher education is instructive in this respect. The binary distinction between universities and polytechnics was abolished by act of parliament in 1992. Yet immediately people started talking of new (1992) and old (pre-1992) universities. There are further distinctions within the 'old' universities between the elite colleges of Oxford and Cambridge, the 1960s campus universities such as Sussex and the 'redbrick' universities of the industrial cities of England. To assert that a degree is worth the same whether is comes from Slough's own much criticised but certainly innovative Thames Valley University or from Oxford is patently absurd. Large employers will continue to recruit on the place of education rather than the number of GCSE passes or the class of degree an applicant has.

These distinctions between universities articulate with distinctions between schools, since so much of university admissions policy is based on 'A' level results. Quite clearly the student from the private school, or even the state school in the leafy suburbs, is much more likely to get high grades than the student from the inner city comprehensive. It is easier to recruit and keep good staff. Teaching groups are smaller, buildings and equipment are often more up-to-date.

Morris is interested in education in two separate ways, neither of which has much to do with the continuing role of education as social selector. Firstly, as a practising craftsman, he was very concerned with the quality of the young craftsperson, and the need to maintain a lively creativity in young people. This has had a continuing influence on English education, as we shall see in chapter nine which describes some work done in rural Oxfordshire schools directly influenced by Morris. Secondly, Morris was concerned to 'make Socialists', with the processes by which the working-class could educate its own members for its own purposes. This too remains a lively debate in English adult education, with a significant strand of work done in trade unions and community organisations, occasionally with the support of more formal educational bodies such as local authority adult education services, university departments of continuing education or the Workers' Educational Association.

Eton College, sandwiched between Slough and Windsor, is a key link between educational privilege, and economic and political power. In his 1992 *Essential Anatomy of Britain*, Anthony Sampson, heroic chronicler of the British establishment, exclaims that there were 'only' two Eton men in the Cabinet, plus the Governor of the Bank of England.[39] Enough, surely. In any case this seems to have been a low point. As ever, Patrick Keiller offers his own particular spin on this in 'Robinson in Space': by the time Douglas Hurd went to work at the National Westminster Bank, there were 'only' three Old Etonians in a cabinet of twenty-three. In describing the domination of cabinets of all political shades by Old Etonians between 1868 and 1955, and subsequent decline, he suggests that 'either Eton is no longer what it was or, more likely, government is no longer an occupation that is so necessary for old Etonians to bother about.' The implication is that they are far too busy making their fortunes in the de-regulated post-Thatcher economy.

---

39. Anthony Sampson, *The essential anatomy of Britain: democracy in crisis* (Hodder and Stoughton, 1992)

It was from the apex of the elite system that Queen Victoria successfully kept the peasants out of Windsor Great Park and thus created the need for a wide detour on the Thames path. Eton College was involved in a similar, though unsuccessful, episode in the 1980s. Marion Shoard, so long the champion of public access to the British countryside, takes up the story in her splendid and timely book, *A Right to Roam* (1999):

> ...when Berkshire County Council discovered that the Environment Agency intended to build a new flood relief channel between Maidenhead and Datchet to reduce flood risk in Maidenhead, it stepped in to ensure that public paths were established along the entire length. The path creation process went smoothly until Eton College objected to a half-mile stretch on the edge of their grounds because it would erode their privacy. The College proposed that along that stretch the path should be switched from the southern to the northern side of the channel. Berkshire County Council opposed this idea as it would have placed the path between the new flood channel and the M4 — a far less appealing situation than the one they had originally proposed, which provided views of the relief channel on one side and trees, playing fields, and college grounds on the other. The county council's view was supported by the inspector at a public inquiry and subsequently by the Secretary of State for the Environment in 1994; the way was clear for the path to be open.[40]

However, this decision probably does not indicate the imminent downfall of privilege...

There is a state school in the borough of Slough which calls itself Slough and Eton School, but this is largely Asian. It is in the unusual position of being a Church of England school, with a largely Muslim student body and Sikh governors. It is certainly a compelling move from friendly, workaday Slough a mile down the road to Eton, where the college boys are wandering around in the main

---

40. Marion Shoard, *A right to roam* (Oxford University Press, 1999) p.232

street in their striped trousers, tail-coats and white bow-ties. The irony is that parents in Slough are just as keen on the subtle distinctions of educational establishments as those who send their sons to Eton. Slough is one of the last strongholds of the selective secondary grammar school in England, and local parents have long opposed any tinkering with this system, despite the fact that it condemns a majority of their children to attend second class schools. Paul Sohal, born in India and a Slough councillor for ten years from 1989-99, told me that Asian parents are especially keen to preserve the grammar schools. The percentage of Asian and other ethnic minority students at Slough's grammar schools is just as high as it is at the town's other secondary schools, even without taking account of the fact that one of the grammar schools is Roman Catholic and therefore largely white. As with all immigrant and refugee communities, a high value is placed on education as a way of individual advancement. The fact that the advancement of some is going to be at the expense of others, and that even their advancement is still not going to place them on a level with students in private schools — all this seems to be laid aside for the moment.

Meanwhile Slough suffers from the managed inequalities of an unequal and unfair society. Even within the town, facilities in some largely Asian neighbourhoods are worse than in other largely white areas. Even the roads tell the same story. In the old county of Berkshire, facilities were worse in Slough than in smarter towns such as Maidenhead and Newbury. At least the current Labour MP, Fiona McTaggart, has come to live in the town — her Conservative predecessor preferred Ascot. But her government does not at the moment appear to have any large plan to reduce inequality, even if it is keen to put a more humane face upon it. For Paul Sohal, the day-to-day business of trying to make small improvements in the lives of his constituents must have seemed a long way from his political roots in the Indian 'land-grab' movement, supporting landless peasants in taking direct action to acquire land on which to grow their own food. Then in the 1970s he was active in the trade union movement.

Morris had ample time and space to observe the inequalities of Victorian London, even to contrast his own life as a successful businessman with that of the workers he addressed at public meetings or stood shoulder-to-shoulder with at often violent demonstrations. But he also had a model of a more equal and, to him, morally superior life: Iceland. Morris visited Iceland twice, in 1871 and 1873. I am certainly not denying that those trips had a strong emotional significance for Morris. Put bluntly, they enabled him to avoid a situation in the family life, namely Jane's affair with the 'other' resident of Kelmscott Manor, Dante Gabriel Rossetti, which he clearly found himself unable to confront directly. However, as Fiona MacCarthy emphasises, they also suggested to him 'a more positive political direction':

> It was in Iceland, seeing life lived at the barest limits of survival, that Morris learned the lesson he turned into a tenet of political intransigence over the next decade: 'that the most grinding poverty is a trifling evil compared to the inequality of classes'.[41]

At the same time, Morris must have been aware that simply sharing in the same grinding poverty as one's neighbours is not an attractive advertisement for socialism. Besides, as MacCarthy points out, the Icelanders for the most part had built lives characterised by 'dignity, productiveness and poetry'. Again, it is the moral case against capitalism that is uppermost in Morris's mind. It is also important in both Morris and in contemporary life that there is a strong case for reducing the total amount we consume. If shared grinding poverty is unattractive, so too is the American way of life, which involves consuming per

---

41. MacCarthy, p.276

capita a far greater share of the world's resources than other nations, while contributing equally unfairly to the sum total of global pollution and global warming. The simple fact that the majority of the inhabitants of the United States are overweight speaks for itself. Morris certainly believed in the potential for human happiness implicit in a simpler and more leisurely way of life (an argument we shall develop in the next chapter), and in the need to support poorer countries in their hour of need, as through the Iceland Relief Fund during the famine of 1882.

The truth of the matter is that we have not managed as a society, as a collective whole, to answer those questions the Greeks first asked themselves about what constitutes 'the good life' and how within that context an individual can live 'a good life'. It is enlightening, but no more than a beginning, to consider the abundant life of those well-known lines from William Blake's *Jerusalem*:

> I will not cease from mental fight,
> Nor shall my sword sleep in my hand,
> Till we have built Jerusalem,
> In England's green and pleasant land.

Blake is hard to understand. As E.P. Thompson has made clear, there is a complex theological argument about the location of God within each human being at the centre of Blake's world which came down to him from the general dissenting tradition, which we saw a little of in the previous chapter. Thompson places great stress on the poem 'In the divine image' (from *Songs of Innocence*):

> For Mercy has a human heart
> Pity, a human face:
> And love, the human form divine,
> And Peace, the human dress.

Thompson comments:

> If God exists in men (sic) and nowhere else, then the whole cosmic conflict between darkness and light, things

corporeal and spiritual, must be enacted within oneself and one's fellow men and nowhere else.[42]

A strange result of the very difficulty of Blake is that members of the Conservative and Labour parties seem equally at home singing Blake's 'Jerusalem', as do the Women's Institute and Last Night at the Proms audiences at London's Albert Hall. The BBC's James Naughtie refers to it yearly as Blake's 'great hymn to social justice'. The truth is, of course, that none of those bodies has a clearly defined view of what Jerusalem looks like, let alone a programme for achieving it. On the one hand the 'green and pleasant' land plays too easily into the hands of the those for whom England is a fanciful pre-industrial land of rural landscapes, concerned landlords and respectful peasants. On the other hand, it has a new resonance for those who believe that the 'greening' of our society is the only way to achieve a sustainable balance between human beings and their natural environment. As Edmund Wilson rightly pointed out, imagination and common-sense are required to work out the details of Utopia. At this stage in the journey up the Thames, I am certain of only one thing: that neither Windsor nor Slough are blueprints for Jerusalem.

---

42. E.P. Thompson, *Witness against the beast: William Blake and the moral law* (Cambridge University Press, 1993) pp.159/60

Chapter 5
Cookham: a very English village?

I would like about half a dozen homes in which I was 'father' in each one, and similar nonsense. (Stanley Spencer)

Copulation is worse than beastly unless it takes place as the result of natural desire and kindliness on both sides. (William Morris)

The royal river ends at Windsor. The social conflicts of Runnymede and Windsor are firstly between the crown and the nobility and secondly between the nobility and the common people. For much of the rest of this book we shall be concerned with more familiar conflicts between those who live in relative comfort on the basis of the ownership of land, houses and salaries, and those who depend on jobs and wages and the occasional hand-out from the state to get by on a daily basis. Whether in town or country, social division is the daily reality of English life. In his already classic study of the contested notion of Englishness in the context of the deserted village of Tyneham on the Isle of Purbeck in Dorset, Patrick Wright refers to the 'rural class structure that had shaped every detail of life, and squeezed vast canyons of social distance into that tiny English valley.'[43] I doubt if the canyons were deeper in Tyneham than they are in London, Oxford or Cookham.

But the river still has its surprises. Between Dorney and Bray, only five miles beyond Windsor, the M4 crosses the river and heads south before circling in a wide loop around Reading, the largest of the towns on the river. At Maidenhead, the A4, the old coaching road from London to Bath

---

43. Patrick Wright, *The village that died for England: the strange story of Tyneham* (Jonathan Cape, 1995) p.344

and Bristol, and the Great Western Railway also strike out across the river heading almost due west. The crossing is accomplished by one of Brunel's most elegant bridges, the longest single brick span in Europe and the subject of Turner's painting 'Rain, steam and speed.' Meanwhile, the Thames pursues its own course north as far as Bourne End before turning west through Marlow to Henley and then south into Reading through its pleasant riverine suburb of Caversham. Naturally, the river itself does the detour in reverse — it is the traveller heading west along the Thames whose route follows the directions indicated here. However, this northern extension of the Thames, sitting beneath the steep, wooded slopes of the Chiltern Hills, is a backwater which has acquired considerable social status over the years. 'Robinson', in his film tour of England, notes that there are no factories between Heathrow and Reading.

Opposite Cookham itself is the Cliveden Estate. Cliveden is both beautiful and unfortunate, as Mari Pritchard and Humphrey Carpenter describe in their book *A Thames Companion*, a mine of useless but fascinating information.[44] Its first owner, George Villiers, the dissolute Duke of Buckingham, killed the Earl of Shrewsbury in a duel here, watched by his lover Lady Shrewsbury. In the 1930s the house was in the hands of the Astor family and the 'Cliveden set' were accused of plotting appeasement with Nazi Germany. Despite handing the house over to the National Trust in 1942, the Astors continued to live at Cliveden and entertaining in the 1950s was just as sumptuous as in the inter-war years. In the 1960s Cliveden became notorious once more as the scene of sex scandals which more than anything created the mood of general 'time for a change' disgust that brought down the Conservative government in 1964. These events centred on the riverside cottage which Stephen Ward rented from

44. Mari Pritchard and Humphrey Carpenter, *A Thames companion* (Oxford Illustrated Press, 1976)

Lord Astor for £1 a year. It was here that Ward entertained friends such as John Profumo, the Secretary of State for War, a Russian diplomat and their shared sex partner, Christine Keeler.

Henley has remained the rowing capital of the Thames, and is an integral part of the London 'season', along with 'Royal' Ascot, Wimbledon and the Lord's test match. More prosaically, the branch lines from Maidenhead to Bourne End and Marlow and from Twyford to Henley mean that this is prime commuting country, a pleasant alternative to the 'stockbroker' belt of Surrey, with the river always at hand for exercise and entertainment. Boulter's Lock, between Maidenhead and Cookham is one of the largest and busiest locks on the river, as it has been since Victorian times. With the coming of the railways, the river was seen increasingly as a recreational resource, and between 1870 and 1914, Cliveden Reach was an epicentre of fashionable leisure. Thus the crowded bustle of Stanley Spencer's paintings of the river are based on the continuing popularity of the river. However, the sleek punts that Spencer depicted massing around Cookham Bridge in 'Christ preaching at Cookham Regatta' have largely been replaced by squat cabin cruisers.

By contrast with Marlow, Henley or even Bourne End, Cookham is tiny. That it has achieved fame at all is largely down to one man, the painter Stanley Spencer (1891-1959). That England is a land of painters comes as something of a surprise to those who think of high culture as a predominantly 'foreign' phenomenon. It is true that England did not produce the wealth of mediaeval paintings which Flanders produced or the great Renaissance art of Italy. When the pre-Raphaelites looked back to the painters 'before Raphael' it was to continental European models they looked. William Morris's exultation of the art of the Middle Ages is based above all on architecture, the only art form for which there was still abundant evidence in the great cathedrals, the humbler village churches and secular buildings such as bridges and barns. The elite sta-

100

tus of the arts in England and their foreignness go hand in hand. The logical outcome is the current position, in which the Royal Opera House has consistently received the largest of all public arts subsidies for musical plays produced mainly in foreign languages. On the few occasions when an English opera is put on (for example, the works of Benjamin Britten or Michael Tippett) prices are usually lower to reflect the reduced demand for seats. Opera in English does not have the social 'cachet' of opera in Italian, French or German. English music, like English painting, is often seen as narrow and parochial. It remains to be seen whether this position may alter much under the new regime at the rebuilt Opera House in Covent Garden. As a condition of the expenditure of large amounts of public money, the company is committed to greater public access, but it will certainly be access to an elitist, minority notion of 'culture'.

Stanley Spencer was born at the right moment to be an English painter. He studied at the Slade School in the years immediately before the First World War among a generation of students who included Eric Wadsworth, Paul Nash, David Bomberg and William Roberts. While much of his studies concentrated on the great work of the early Italian painters, he was also open to the contemporary European influences crowding into London at that time. Two of his drawings were included in the 1912 Second Post-Impressionist exhibition alongside works by Wyndham Lewis, Vanessa Bell, Matisse, Picasso and Cezanne. But if the freedom of form and expression come from post-Impressionism, the feeling for the human form as the central content of painting and for the public nature of art come from the Italian middle ages. A similar duality between Modernism and Classicism can be observed in the work of Hilda Carline, Spencer's first wife, who grew up in a family of painters and attended the Slade in the years immediately after the First World War.

But Cookham, rather than standing as a symbol of the inter-connectedness of England and Europe, has come to stand for a certain view of England and Englishness.

Patrick Wright writes of the deserted village of Tyneham in Dorset: 'It was reborn as a perfect English village of the mind, one that belongs on the same map as Stanley Spencer's Cookham.'[45] I liked Cookham the first time I saw it. Superficially it has not changed. Many features of the present village can be easily recognised from Spencer's paintings. These include the iron bridge across the river, the flint and stone church, the High Street with its shops and houses, including Fernlea, the Victorian white-painted brick semi where Spencer spent both the early and later parts of his life, and the National Trust-protected Moor, a common in all but name. The most obvious change is the Methodist Chapel at the river end of the High Street which has become the Stanley Spencer Gallery. It has a comfortingly traditional red phone-box crouching up against its walls. It is another of Patrick Wright's emblems of English culture. For him, the traditional telephone kiosk has an emblematic fascination and is a symbol of the continuity of ideas of public service broken by the privatisation mania of the Thatcher years: 'Hiding against rough weather in the old red telephone box was the petrified spirit of the Welfare State itself.'[46]

Yet the image of stability is false and misleading. The catalogue for the 1997 Washington exhibition for which Fiona MacCarthy produced her essay 'Stanley Spencer, English visionary'[47] has a photo of Spencer himself leaving Mrs Mackay's shop in the High Street clutching a loaf and shopping bag in one hand and a cauliflower in the other. Senior Service cigarettes, Wall's ice-cream and Brooke Bond tea are on sale, while an inverted box of Fray Bentos corned beef from Argentina suggests the international basis on which the health and welfare of English villages already depended. But where could you buy corned beef or

45. Wright, *The village that died for England*, p.35
46. Wright, *A journey through ruins*, pp.187/8
47. Fiona MacCarthy, *Stanley Spencer, English visionary* (Yale University Press, 1997)

cauliflowers in the village today? Almost all of the remaining shops are expensive little boutiques. The only one selling food is a delicatessen called 'Ciao Bello', its discrete window display still contained within the original casement windows. The only Spencer at large in the village appears to be the hairdresser Daniel Spencer, whose shop shares with Ciao Bello the mellow brick house with the Cookham Goldsmith iron sign hanging above the front door. This is shopping for the discerning middle-classes, not for a 'rural village' in any meaningful sense of either word. As if to make the point, the mock Tudor 'big house' facing onto the rich green turf of the Moor, Moor Hall, is now the headquarters of the Institute of Marketing.

The very concept of marketing is a potent symbol of a society which seems to find it difficult to fulfil people's basic needs for work, shelter and healthy food, but all too easy to create 'markets' for the most unimaginable of nicknacks and luxury goods. It is precisely William Morris's point — that capitalism is an economic system which creates needs to ensure its own survival rather than responding to human need and consequently ensuring the survival of the species. And of course it is a further reminder that Morris himself found it easier to create a market for his luxury household furnishings than to 'sell' the revolution to the dispossessed of England. 'Robinson' notes the presence of the Institute of Marketing at Cookham but reserves for Portsmouth his judgement on the economy of these areas of Southern England which while clearly 'not London' can only be understood in the context of London's existence:

> (The British eighteenth century navy) on whose supremacy was built the capitalism of land, finance and commercial services, centred on the City of London, which dominates the economy of the South of England. Those of us aesthetes who view the passing of the visible industrial economy with regret and who long for an authenticity of appearance based on manufacturing and innovative modern design are inclined to view this English culture as a

bizarre and damaging anachronism but if so it is not an unsuccessful one.[48]

It might also be noted that, if shopping in Cookham has become a rarefied activity, the village shows little sign of productive economy either. Brewing, tanning, lace-making and milling have all been carried on here in the past. Now only the names of some houses — Tannery House, Brew House, The Maltings, Ovey's Farm — betray signs of an industrious past. The Old Forge is now a restaurant. In like fashion, the chemist's shop has reverted in very recent times to being a private house, its name, 'The Old Apothecary', seeming to mock anyone who still expects to be able to obtain the basics of life in the village. Perhaps it is best not to be too critical of Cookham, for the trends at work here are only an extreme example of the prettification and gentrification which is the lot of most Thames valley villages. Paul Barker in an entertaining *New Statesman* sketch on 24 October 1997 described how a milkman had delivered to one High Street cottage a pint of semi-skimmed milk and four plastic bottles of mineral water. He continued: 'When Spencer wanted to paint the baptism of Christ, he set it in a local swimming pool. Today he could baptise Christ from a plastic bottle.' To be honest, there is little to connect smart new Cookham with the shabby, comfortable village of the 1920s and '30s when Spencer was painting here. Such links exist at the level of superficial similarities and myth rather than of real life. Oddly, Barker notes the overgrown privet hedge outside Fernlea as an intrusion into the smart 'new' Cookham, without mentioning Spencer's drawing for the 1927 Chatto and Windus almanac on display in the Gallery. It shows a man (probably Stanley's brother Sydney) cutting the same impossibly overgrown privet hedge. Privet was ever thus.

---

48. Patrick Keiller, 'Robinson in Space' (BBC/British Film Institute, 1997)

In one sense, it is extraordinary the way artists who have been influenced to a significant degree by international movements (Morris, Spencer) come to be identified as uniquely 'English' artists. But equally they can be seen as part-and-parcel of the internationalisation of England, firstly as Britain and then as the British Empire and Commonwealth. Earlier than most countries England had to begin the long process of coming to terms with the dual nature of globalisation — its tendency to make things the same (epitomised in popular music or in international brands such as Coca Cola) and at the same time the psychological urge it manifests to emphasise difference. While difference in the year 2000 is conceived of most often in terms of particular cultural formations based on ethnicity, sexual preference, tastes in music, films and food, its first manifestation is in the emphasis on the specificity of place. A country not caught up in globalisation processes feels no need to assert its difference, because those differences are simply the contents of daily life.

So it is precisely at the point when the British Empire was at its peak at the close of the nineteenth century that the sense of England as a 'special', unique sort of place comes to importance. Precisely at the moment English art is taken seriously internationally, it asserts its Englishness. For Morris the sense of place comes in the carefully located scenes of *News from Nowhere* or the precise references to the natural history of the Thames valley in his fabric and wallpaper designs. In the case of Spencer it is narrowed down to the few miles around his lifelong home in Cookham. Similar comments about the significance of place could be made about Thomas Hardy and Dorset in literature or about Elgar, Vaughan Williams and the Welsh Marches in music. So Morris moves us from the internationalism of Gothic to the Englishness of Arts and Crafts; Spencer from the cosmopolitan modernism of post-Impressionism to a view of Cookham as a summation of both the natural and divine worlds.

That England is a land of poets, painters and musicians is no longer in doubt, at least for those people with a real love of live culture, both popular and classical. Yet the point of art is surely to refer to a sphere beyond everyday experience, a domain which cuts across the limitations of time and space. That Spencer is a visionary painter is certain. That Spencer is an 'English' visionary is less certain, unless one uses English in the most banal way to state where he comes from and to say something about his subject matter. It is not at all clear why we should see Spencer as so very English when we emphasise the international value of Italian painters such as Leonardo and Michelangelo. It is curious and interesting to contrast the life of Spencer's contemporary Picasso, who is diversely described as French (he lived most of his life in France), as Spanish (he was born there and much of his iconography refers to Spanish culture) or Catalan (he spent his formative artistic years in Barcelona). We would agree, I think, that it doesn't matter much. And yet it does matter in the case of Spencer...

Spencer's Englishness cannot be separated altogether from his religious nature. And in that sense he is in danger of being herded into a pretty unholy alliance which includes T.S. Eliot, the Englishman from Missouri, and D.H. Lawrence, the Englishman from Nottingham who spent the second half of his life being almost anywhere on the face of the earth that was definitely not England. It is easy to be rude or cynical about Spencer's religion. It is English not only because he says it is, but in its vagueness, its soft and sentimental focus, its total lack of interest in issues of dogma. For people of the year 2000, accustomed to think of religion as a relic of the pre-modern period, it seems an anachronism. Yet towards the end of the century, one of the most noticeable features of social life was not only a new interest in the local, the specific, the national, but also a new interest in religion of all kinds. There was much talk in the 1990s of the threat of a new fundamentalism, visible on the one hand in the rise of Islam in countries such as Iran, Libya, Algeria and Palestine but also in the strength of fundamentalist Protestant churches in the U.S.A. and their missionary outposts in Central and South America. Christian fundamentalism is neo-liberal in economics, profoundly conservative in its views on 'a woman's place', fanatical in its opposition to abortion. Its attraction is that it asserts rather than argues, and so is able to offer certainty rather than those two characteristics of our times — doubt and uncertainty.

What then of the actual beliefs of Stanley Spencer? Stanley Spencer denied there was anything particularly special about religion, or the fusion of religion, sex and daily life in his paintings. As Fiona MacCarthy writes in her essay on Spencer:

> The 'Bible life', in the sense of daily habit rather than externally imposed discipline, permeated the house and Spencer as a boy accepted it unquestioningly: 'Somehow religion was something to do with me, and I was to do with religion. It came into my vision naturally, like the sky and rain.' He absorbed this religiousness into the bloodstream. It affected his language; Spencer wrote, as he spoke, in a curious mixture of the Biblical and slangy. 'Do you know what good art is?', he once asked his friend and director of the Tate gallery, John Rothenstein. 'It's just saying "ta" to God.' His perception of Christ was of an Almighty Artist, creating works of charity and faith and love.[49]

I am not convinced that we should believe every one of the many, many words that Spencer confided to his diaries. Like many great artists, some of his most personal writing seems like a conscious effort to throw critics off the scent. We know that Spencer was intensely interested in religion and read widely about it. He knew about Islam as well as about Christianity. It seems unlikely that 'saying "ta" to God' stands up as either a summary of his views on art, or as a statement of his personal theology. Perhaps it is wiser to stick to the paintings and I would begin with another

---

49. MacCarthy, *Stanley Spencer, English visionary*, p.8

hedge picture, "Neighbours" of 1936. This is in the Gallery in Cookham and a useful little gallery guide explains that 'the composition is based on a childhood memory of his elder sister Annie in the garden of the family home Fernlea exchanging gifts over the hedge with her cousin next door.'[50] The gift is a bunch of red tulips which both female figures stretch upwards towards, a movement symbolic of both physical and spiritual communion. This is also the period of Spencer's explicit sexual paintings which have for subject the painter himself and Patricia Preece, who was to become his second wife. But there are more tulips left in the garden, as a clear indication that the riches of the earth are best enjoyed and multiplied by sharing them. This picture, more than the sexually explicit nudes of the period, seems to sum up Spencer's approach to relationships — the sharing of the material world, the exchange of bodily fluids in sex acts, the reciprocity of the human and the divine. Where the nudes display post-coital isolation, the cousins demonstrate connectedness.

Spencer's scrapbooks, some of which are on display at Cookham, demonstrate his consummate draughtsmanship and ability to add a 'divine' spark to the most ordinary of activities. There is a touch of Blake here, the Blake who believed that 'everything that moves is holy', and Blake the draughtsman — for example the ecstatic sweeping forms in the pencil preparatory drawing for the great unfinished picture of Christ preaching at Cookham Regatta which dominates the small Gallery.

An attachment to the mundane and the everyday breeds a capacity for endurance and this is best demonstrated by Spencer's paintings from both World Wars. Spencer paints not the horror of war and its futility, which should be commonplace to anyone who has thought seriously about the subject, but the comfort of small repeated actions which give meaning in a situation which in itself is devoid of

50. Carolyn Leder, *The Barbara Karmel bequest catalogue* (Stanley Spencer Gallery, 1996)

sense. Not the 'meanings' imposed by intellectual systems (science, Marxism, whatever), but the meanings that derive from everyday life: open, shared, democratic, public. We all make meaning all the time, looking for patterns in our own lives and in those of other people. Both of these sets of war paintings take us from Cookham. First we go through the woods and commons of Berkshire, past the atomic sites of Aldermaston and Greenham Common, to the village of Burghclere, the unexpected setting for the Sandham Memorial Chapel, which houses Spencer's paintings of the First World War. Spencer saw active service for four years, including two years in Macedonia as a medical orderly. It is the first really cold day of autumn, fading into winter. There are hedges of sloe, acorns, beech-nuts, hips and haws — a cornucopia of nature. And by complete contrast the first of the winter flowering gorse grows here; the same gorse which still flowers on Putney Heath where the Swedish botanist Linnaeus saw it two hundred years ago and remarked that it was one of the great wonders of nature. The trees outside the chapel (a mediocre building of red brick) are apple-trees, the apples of a painterly redness and roundness, looking like nothing so much as Spencer's own painted apples in his picture 'The Apple Gatherers' in the Tate Gallery.

The murals celebrate the daily life of the soldiers but are also what he calls 'a mixture of real and spiritual fact'. The beautifully written and recently republished National Trust guide book by Duncan Robinson[51] emphasises that 'Spencer regarded the mundane activities of the hospital with a sense of religious ritual, and the hospital pictures symbolise a quotation from St Augustine's Confessions: '...ever busy yet ever at rest, gathering yet never needing; bearing; filling; guarding; creating; nourishing; perfecting.' It is as if the male experience in the war gave some insight into that world of the 'labour of women's hands'

---

51. Duncan Robinson, *Stanley Spencer at Burghclere* (National Trust, 1991)

which so few men have ever taken seriously and which illuminates so many of his domestic pictures. In 1923 he told a group of art students that

> ...ordinary experiences or happenings in life are continu- ally developing and bringing to light all sorts of artistic discoveries... When I scrubbed floors, I would have all sorts of marvellous thoughts, so that at last, when I was fully equipped for scrubbing — bucket, apron and "prayer mat" in hand — I used to feel much the same as if I was going to church.[52]

There is an interesting and, I think, significant link with Morris here, but also a point of divergence. The Revd. F. B. Guy, the tutor who coached Morris for Oxford, where he was to have trained as a priest, had been closely connected with the Oxford Movement, that surge of renewal within the Church of England which had emphasised its Catholic nature and done much to revive interest in church liturgy and ritual. There is little doubt that Morris would have known the hymn by John Keble which includes the words: 'The trivial round, the common task,/ Would furnish all we need to ask'. So far this would serve as a text for both Mor- ris and Spencer. But the next lines 'Room to deny our- selves, a road/ To bring us daily nearer God' is pure Morris, taking up the Oxford Movement themes of self- denial and self-discipline. Penelope Fitzgerald, in her edi- tion of Morris's *'Novel on blue paper'* manuscript (the title is hers, not Morris's) which deals with the love of two brothers for the same woman, even uses Morris's religious training to explain his silent tolerance of the Rossetti-Jane Morris relationship.[53]

It is not my intention to give a detailed account of this extraordinary set of murals, which reflect Spencer's expe- rience of war both as a trainee in a hospital in England

52. In Robinson, p.8
53. William Morris, *The novel on blue paper*, edited and introduced by Penelope Fitzgerald (Journeyman Press, 1982)

and on the Salonika front in Macedonia, but rather to concentrate on the central Resurrection painting which occupies the whole of the wall facing the entrance door, and the upper panels immediately to the left ('Dug-out') and right ('Reveille').

'Dug-out' is a picture of the Salonika front. It is the starkest of all the paintings. The only pattern is provided by the tangled coils of bared wire. Otherwise there is little but bare stone, the soldiers emerging from the trenches depositing their belts and bags as they come. Some of the men gaze up out of their horror towards the picture on the east wall — 'Resurrection'. The size of the painting and the number of figures in it mean that the Christ who receives the crosses from the soldiers is a rather small 'human' figure in the middle distance who shares the suffering of the soldiers. Spencer was later to use the figure of his 'Scarecrow' of 1934 for his 'Crucifixion' of the same year: it is the identification of Christ with the poor and the outsider which reflects the position leading theologians of the 1920s and 1930s were adopting in reaction to mass unemployment and the rise of fascism. There is much shaking of hands as the soldiers appear to offer one another the 'peace' — that which the world has not been able to give them. The whole picture is alarmingly full of physical activity, as if Spencer is saying that the only resurrection worth having is that of the body, preferably with the rest of the created world thrown in for good measure. In 'Reveille', the war is over. The soldiers are dressing and shaving while the news that the war is over spreads. Spencer is a survivor. It is this central experience of death, central to European experience in the twentieth century, which somehow cuts off Spencer from Morris. Morris, let us not forget, was in favour of violent change. He explains very carefully in *News from Nowhere* how the change came about from the world he had lived in to the land of nowhere. The subversive question again arises whether in this sense Morris may not be part of the problem rather than the solution.

Duncan Robinson refers in the guide-book to Spencer's 'decade of introspection' in the '30s. It is also arguably the decade when his over-sized ego tended to come before his love of humanity. Robinson sees the Port Glasgow paintings done by Spencer during the Second World War as the way forward for Spencer:

> There, once again surrounded by teeming, toiling humanity, he rediscovered his affection for his fellows as individual men and women, bound together by their common tasks. 'I felt as disinclined to disturb them', he wrote, 'as I would be to disturb a service in a church.' In many ways Port Glasgow was Spencer's sequel to Burghclere.[54]

This somewhat truncated view of Spencer's development is shared by Fiona MacCarthy, who suggests that Port Glasgow is the logical follow-up to the Burghclere pictures. I think this misses the significance of the pictures of humdrum peacetime life. Spencer makes as many claims for the importance of those ordinary daily activities and scenes as he does for the daily routines of wartime. Indeed, Spencer himself saw the Port Glasgow pictures as being about daily life rather than the exceptional life of wartime. He wrote: 'In each of these cases the place and the feeling it had was an important part of the work I did. They amount to a kind of memorial to these respective places.' For example, Lithgow's shipyard was 'dark and cosy and full of mysterious places and happenings, like a vast Cookham blacksmith's workshop interior.'[55]

* * *

Spencer and Morris were not the only searchers who were intrigued by the 'trivial round, the common task'. Morris had visited Edward Carpenter on his small-holding near Sheffield. Carpenter (1844-1929) was the nineteenth cen-

54. Robinson, p.11
55. In MacCarthy, *Stanley Spencer, English visionary*

tury apostle of the simple life, fellowship and open sexual relations (including homosexuality). Morris wrote to Georgiana Burne-Jones on Christmas Eve, 1884:

> I listened with longing heart to his account of his patch of ground, seven acres: he says that he and his fellow can almost live on it: they grow their own wheat, and send flowers and fruit to Chesterfield and Sheffield markets: all that sounds very agreeable to me. It seems to me that the real way to enjoy life is to accept all its necessary ordinary details and turn them into pleasure by taking interest in them.

Not all the exponents of 'back to nature' were as attractive as Edward Carpenter. On a darker note, Patrick Wright goes into some detail about Rolf Gardiner and his activities centred on the Springhead community in inter-war Dorset, with its roots into the youth movement of the '20s in both Germany and England, and ideas of national renewal, but also emphasising more dubious links with Mosley and Hitler. Wright is ambivalent but emphasises both the 'fellow-travelling' of Gardiner and also the distinctive nature of his vision:

> Gardiner's view was closer to what he called the 'Christian gnosticism' of the seventeenth-century poet Thomas Traherne: he wanted 'not the communism of the sect, but the communion of ordinary men and women in work and art, in their relation with birds, beasts and flowers, stars, trees and men.'[56]

Traherne's work was rediscovered, in a quite literal sense, because many of his works only became known after the recovery of a manuscript from a London bookstall in 1908. He features in a curious book called *The English Spirit: the Little Gidding anthology of English spirituality*, published in 1987 in, of all places, Nashville, Tennessee, a town more known for popular music in general and Elvis

---

56. Wright, *The village that died for England*, p.188

Presley in particular than for spirituality. Traherne writes for example:

> You never enjoy the world aright, till you see how a (grain of) sand exhibiteth the wisdom and power of God: and prize in everything the service which they do you, by manifesting His glory and goodness to your Soul, far more than the visible beauty on their surface, or the material services they can do your body.[57]

But Stanley Spencer wanted it both ways — the physical as an intimation of the divine but also in all its physical attraction.

Whether or not there is anything peculiarly English in English spirituality or whether we are simply dealing with the accident of artists, poets and social thinkers interested in spiritual matters who also happened to be English, is a decision I leave happily to the reader. The connections are certainly there to be made. For example Ralph Vaughan Williams has already been mentioned as a composer with a heightened sense of place. On 14 September 1911, Vaughan Williams' 'Five mystical songs' with words by George Herbert were heard for the first time at that most 'English' of musical events — the Three Choirs Festival in Worcester. The baritone voice rises plaintively above the choir and orchestra in an unmistakable way; the exquisite sound of a narrow, rural vision of England. And curiously the opposite can be true — that spirituality can be internationalist and expansive in outlook, as it is in Tippett's wartime oratorio *A Child of our Time* with its use of American Negro spirituals as a timeless commentary on the time-constrained action of the story.

There is, then, a spiritual and religious strand that winds its way through the scientific disbelief of the twen-

---

57. Thomas Traherne, in (eds) Paul Handley et al, *The English Spirit: the Little Gidding anthology of English spirituality* (Abingdon Press, Nashville,1987) p.120

tieth century. The Enlightenment and modernity are the apotheosis of the classical tradition, taken up by the renaissance. Man is the measure of all things. But science has not delivered the goods. It is not only the pollution and the risks of science which we shall find further upstream at Abingdon, in the next chapter, but the failure to ensure the fair distribution of untold wealth which has given rise to warfare in Europe and far beyond. Yet modernity and irrationalism have a symbiotic hold on one another: for every war launched by greed and inequality, another is carried forward by tribalism, religious and political fanaticism. Again, it is Michael Tippett who springs to mind here, urging us in *A Child of our Time* to recognise and live with our darkness as well as our light, that we may again be whole, whether we understand that in religious or secular terms.

Little attention is paid in this book to Morris as a poet, and I have not found it necessary to discuss the wearisome argument as to whether Morris is one of the 'best' of Victorian poets, or merely shares their tedium, compounded in his case by the extraordinary speed and length of his poetic outpourings. Yet it is interesting to look back to the Morris of *The Earthly Paradise* here. Morris recognised the profound beauty of the world yet also the inbuilt difficulty of human beings to be happy. There is something warm and sympathetic in the complexity of emotion, the sense of the world's fullness and emptiness, of meaning and futility:

Of heaven and hell I have no power to sing,
I cannot ease the burden of your fears,
Or make quick-coming death a little thing,
Or bring again the pleasure of past years,
Nor for my words shall ye forget your tears,
Or hope again for aught that I can say,
The idle singer of an empty day.

Just as Spencer 'made sense' of human life through its everyday detail, so for Morris, the important argument that links religion and politics is about fellowship. Not for Morris the individualism of Protestant thought and its detachment from the material world but the Anglo-Catholicism of Oxford, medievalism and the shared life. There is a contrast too with the Calvinism of Edward Bellamy's authoritarian socialist utopia described in *Looking Backward* (1888), which I shall suggest in the final chapter was the immediate provocation for *News from Nowhere*. This is very plain in *A Dream of John Ball*, as Michael Holzman has pointed out in showing how Morris deals with the 'problem' of the religious-minded socialists 'by claiming that socialism is the true religious force in society'.[58] He quotes the passage in which the John Ball character claims:

> for I say to you that earth and heaven are not two but one; and this one is that which ye know, and are each one of you a part of, to wit, the Holy Church, and in each one of you dwelleth the life of the Church, unless ye slay it. Ah, my brothers, what an evil doom is this, to be an outcast from the Church, to have none to love you and to speak with you, to be without fellowship![59]

John Ball's vision of future bliss includes the transformation of the tithe barn into a communal granary:

> What else shall ye lack when ye lack masters? Ye shall not lack for the fields ye have tilled, nor the houses ye have built, nor the cloth ye have woven; all these shall be yours, and whatso ye will of all that the earth beareth; then shall no man mow the deep grass for another, while his own kine lack cow-meat; and he that seweth shall reap, and the reaper shall eat in the fellowship the harvest that in fellowship he hath won; and he that buildeth a house shall dwell in it with those that he biddeth of his free will; and

---

58. Michael Holzman, 'The encouragement and warning of history: William Morris's A Dream of John Ball', in (eds) F. Boos and C. Silver, *Socialism and the literary artistry of William Morris* (University of Missouri Press, 1990)
59. In Holzman, pp.106/7

the tithe barn shall garner the wheat for all men to eat of when the seasons are untoward and the rain-drift hideth the sheaves in August: and all shall be without money and without price. Faithfully and merrily then shall all men keep the holidays of the Church in peace of body and joy of heart. And man shall help man, and the saints in heaven shall be glad, because men no more fear each other; and the churl shall be ashamed, and shall hide his churlishness till it be gone, and he be no more a churl; and fellowship shall be established in heaven and on earth.

The emphasis on fellowship is what Morris adds to Froissart, whose account of the Peasants' Revolt he follows quite closely in other respects. As Holzman puts it:

Froissart's John Ball asserts the unity of the peasants, a political unity for political ends; Morris's priest calls for 'fellowship' as a way to achieve economic liberation. If fellowship is the solution to the problems of medieval domination, clearly, for Morris, it was also the solution to the agony of nineteenth-century capitalist domination.[60]

* * *

Morris prefers to write about fellowship than about sexuality. Indeed his romances are most notable for their degree of simple human warmth, of friendship rather than sexual passion. When Morris characters make love, they seem to do so because they actually like one another. It was to his friend Charles Faulkner that Morris wrote the words quoted at the beginning of this chapter, in which he linked sex and friendship. Morris, of course, knew a thing or two about sex. As a student in Oxford he was part of a male artistic set that pursued pretty girls, 'stunners', as avidly as they pursued the rarefied world of mediaeval romance and Gothic art. The tale of Morris's marriage to Jane Burden, of her adultery with Dante Gabriel Rossetti and his possible adultery with Aglaia Coronio or even

60. Holzman, p.107

Georgiana Burne-Jones, whose husband Edward, Morris's best friend, was carrying on with Mary Zambaco... It is gruesome and boring, although it tells us much about the double standards of morality by which Victorian men operated. It also tells us a lot about the marginalisation of women as independent beings in Victorian England. The cover photo in this book is a picture by Maria Spartali, who with Coronio and Zambaco made up a trio of free-thinking women in the Victorian Greek community in London. Spartali is much more often referred to as a model to Rossetti and wife to the American photographer William Stillman, than as a fine Pre-Raphaelite painter in her own right.[61] Germaine Greer makes one dismissive reference to her under the heading of 'primitivism'.[62]

But Morris left it to others to write the tale up. He chose other subjects for his poetry and romances, abandoning his only work (the so-called 'Novel on blue paper') which has any real autobiographical content. Morris's path is from religious vocation to artistic vocation and sexual arousal, followed by a lot of art, a lot of business, substantial amounts of politics, and just maybe a little bit of sexual activity on the side. George Bernard Shaw wrote later that 'Morris was a complete fatalist in his attitude towards the conduct of... all human beings where sex was concerned'.[63] This probably underestimates the strength of the emotions in the tangled web of relationships of the early 1870s, the period when Morris and Rossetti acquired a lease on Kelmscott Manor. It was also the period of his 'Novel on blue paper.' The one person to whom he seemed able to unburden himself at this period was Aglaia Coronio, and

61. See also Jan Marsh and Pamela Gerrish Nunn, *Pre-Raphaelite women artists* (Thames and Hudson, 1998)
62. Germaine Greer, *The obstacle race: the fortunes of women painters and their work* (Secker and Warburg, 1979) p.128
63. G.B. Shaw, 'Morris as I knew him', in (ed) May Morris, *William Morris, artist, writer, socialist,* volume 2 (Basil Blackwell, 1936). Separate edition, William Morris Society, 1996.

he wrote to her the most significant letter of this period on 25 November 1872:

> When I said there was no (real) cause for my feeling low, I meant that my friends had not changed at all towards me in any way and that there had been no quarrelling: and indeed I am afraid it comes from some cowardice or unmanliness in me.

Having made this admission, he launches into a bitter attack on his friend and business partner Rossetti:

> another quite selfish business is that Rossetti has set himself down at Kelmscott as if he never meant to go away; and not only does that keep me away from that harbour of refuge... but also he has all sorts of ways so unsympathetic with the sweet simple old place, that I feel his presence there as a kind of slur on it.

Morris is ready to escape even further — a second trip to Iceland: 'I know clearer now perhaps than then what a blessing & help last year's journey was to me; or what horrors it saved me from.'

If sexuality takes a back seat in Morris's life and art, it seems by contrast that Spencer was only able to place sexuality in a central position in his art by making a pig's ear of his private life. He abandoned what seems like a happy and successful marriage to Hilda Carline, a fine painter herself, for a second 'marriage' to a lesbian neighbour, Patricia Preece, in Cookham. The 'marriage', not surprisingly, did not survive the honeymoon, a performance in which Preece's lesbian partner played a central role as preferred bed-mate of the bride. Where Morris seems to stand aside creatively from his sexual life, Spencer brings the drama of his own sexuality and relationships to frontstage. The double nude portrait of Spencer and Preece, painted in 1937 and now in the Tate Gallery, is central to the plot. Both male and female figures flaunt their genitals yet there is no hint of union between them. The uncooked leg of mutton which has given this picture its unofficial sub-title seems just as likely to initiate erotic activity as the man or the woman. For once Spencer's writing seems to get it right: 'There is in it male, female and animal flesh.' It is hard to believe that such a lifeless painting was done in the same year as the Leeds picture of 'Hilda, Unity and dolls', with its complex emotions between child and dolls, mother and child and artist, ex-wife and daughter.

It is difficult to know exactly what was going on in Spencer's mind in 1937. It is at this point in his life that he toyed in his writings with the idea of polygamy — the line quoted at the head of this chapter. Where some of the later Spencer paintings suggest an atmosphere of free love, of unfettered coupling and uncoupling in which both sexes join with complete equality, such writing suggests merely another variation on male egotism. It is at this point that Morris comes back into the frame, for despite the relatively conventional gender roles in *News from Nowhere*, Morris does mark a shift in Victorian attitudes to both sexual activity and gender roles. While women in Morris's work remain subject to male authority, they perform a much wider range of tasks than would have been conventional in Victorian England, and seem much more likely to take the sexual initiative. These nuances are significant, even if one hundred years later we are sometimes more conscious of the continuities between Morris and his contemporaries than the differences.

At the same time (and here there is a very clear contrast with Spencer), the eroticism which Fiona MacCarthy has recognised in Morris's work is balanced by an equally apparent tendency to prurience. The linking of nudity to innocence goes back to creation myths and the Garden of Eden. Yet there is also a sense in which nudity must be justified: the Bible depicts Adam and Eve as 'properly' naked but the drunken appearance of an unclothed Noah as improper. On the extremes of radical thought in the 1640s and 1650s, nakedness acquires a symbolic value as the casting off of the vanities of the world, an extreme form of the better-known simplicity of dress of the Quakers and other Puritan groups. For Blake, innocence and nakedness belong together. But what is sexually arousing is the suggestion of the forbidden nature of nudity and the voyeuristic pose of the viewer. I am thinking of the prurient interest in young people in dubiously justified states of undress in Victorian artistic/erotic photos, in illustrated editions of Kingsley's *Water Babies*, and in Rackham's illustrations. A similar prurience surfaces in Morris's late novels. Birdalone, in *The Waters of the Wondrous Isles*, manages to spend an extraordinary amount of time naked in the waters rather than clothed upon the isles. Immediately after disrobing to put on their special garments for bathing in the holy well in *The Well at the World's End*, Ralph and Ursula strip off again for a dip in the nearby sea. But the prurience is cyclical, and we are all creatures of our times. In many respects, the heroines of Morris's romances such as Birdalone and Ursula are strong, resilient women who challenge Victorian conventions about how women should behave.

The question remains whether, despite the 'sexual revolution' of the second half of the twentieth century, we are any closer in modern Britain to expressing in our relationships both the solidarity between men and women as equal human beings and the sexual pleasures of intimacy, at ease with our bodies but also aware of their use as instruments of both power and pleasure. Many people now choose to live alone. While at one level, sexual intimacy seems so universal an activity, relationships seem increasingly hard to sustain, whether inside or outside marriage, whether heterosexual or lesbian and gay. The sexual revolution of the 1960s, like most revolutions, has produced unintended and unwanted results. While enabling many men and women to live more honest, open lives, it has all too often shaded off into pornography, violence and the abuse of women and children. Seen in this light, there is much to be said for the view that Spencer's erotic, self-centred pictures of the 1930s are a 'loss of direction' in his moral seriousness and concern for the morality of everyday life as expressed in both the Burghclere pictures and the Port Glasgow pictures.

Perhaps the answer here is that sex in all its forms needs to resume its place as a 'normal' part of social life, neither something to be ashamed of nor something to be in awe of; something to be desired as one part of the 'good' life. The average person's sexuality has never been, and is never likely to be, of interest to Freud and his followers. Yet this is what happens to Spencer in the 1930s — the obstinate obsessiveness of the heterosexual man marrying the lesbian woman. In his later pictures, there is a sense in which sex, like religion in Morris, becomes part of fellowship again, and fellowship is based in the here and now of the material world. And that fellowship begins in work, as in Port Glasgow. In that, at least, Morris and Spencer are at one. It is to the changing world of work that we turn in the next chapter, in which the Thames Valley becomes, for just a little while, "Silicon Valley".

Chapter 6
Reading and Work

A map of the world that does not include Utopia is not worth even glancing at. (Oscar Wilde)

...it is the allowing machines to be our masters and not our servants that so injures the beauty of life nowadays. (William Morris, *How we live and how we might live*)

"If you are finally going to say to an increasing number of people that they are simply surplus to requirements, that they are not really necessary in this society, at that point the basic question returns, of what people need to produce and how they need to produce it and how, over and above all this, they relate to each other while they are producing it". (Raymond Williams)[64]

As a means of promoting human life and happiness, capitalism doesn't work. (Dinah Livingstone)[65]

At the Madejski Stadium

Reading is the largest town that we have visited so far in retracing William Morris's journey up the Thames from Kelmscott House to Kelmscott Manor. Morris ignores Reading and it is easy to see why: Reading has grown extensively on the south bank of the river, but it is only in visiting the smaller suburb of Caversham, or in attending one of the open air music festivals on the riverbank site, that the visitor really encounters the Thames. Most modern travellers, passing through Reading on the M4 motorway, will scarcely

---

64. 'William Morris, questions of work and democracy', interview with Raymond Williams, *William Morris today*, catalogue of the 1984 ICA exhibition, pp.122-125. Part of the interview, recorded on 16 December 1982, was used in a Channel 4 film, *Memories of the future: William Morris*
65. *Work*, an anthology edited by Dinah Livingstone, (Katabasis, 1999) p.297

be aware of Reading as a riverine town at all. Yet Reading is central to my concerns in writing this book and exploring how England has changed in the one hundred years since Morris's death. In particular it provides important evidence on a theme close to Morris's heart — how we organise the work of society and the role of technology in work.

If the M4 traveller is not aware of the Thames at Reading, he or she will certainly be struck, especially if travelling east towards London, by an extraordinary new building which has emerged very recently among the confusion of factories, warehouses and road-works between Reading and Junction 15 (the road to Basingstoke). Vast, metallic, with striking panels of primary colour illuminating the surrounding waste land, the Madejski stadium feels like 'real architecture' compared with the temporary and provisional feel of most of the buildings in the area — factories, a brewery, warehouses, offices, joky supermarkets in the poorest of poor post-modern taste. The Madejski looks as if it's there to last.

The general atmosphere of the stadium on a non-match occasion is one of 'corporate cool' — an immense paved Reception area with air-conditioning, a high ceiling and splendid views over the surrounding mud which should be a one hundred and fifty-bed hotel by the time this book is published. It is interesting to contrast these first impressions with the public turnstiles and their warning notice: 'Prohibited articles — glasses, glass bottles, drink cans, gas canisters, smoke canisters, tools, knives, darts, fireworks, flags and banners, large radio sets, cameras, articles likely to cause injury.' The lad working in the stadium shop explains to me that they're 'pretty lenient' about flags and banners. He clarifies nonchalantly that the real purpose is to keep racist material out of the stadium. The Madejski, then, gives contradictory messages. If one is about the excitement and dangers of popular culture, the other is about the power of money, hospitality suites, and not least the thirty million pounds that John Madejski, the Chairman and sponsor of Reading FC and of all this effort, raised through the sale of his publishing empire, built initially on the success of the

Auto Trader magazine). Yet the two are linked, as it was precisely in the circumstances of industrial nineteenth century urban society that organised leisure grew. Mass production generated mass leisure. And as Ken Worpole points out, it grew up in such a way as to effectively sideline many of the cultural concerns of men like William Morris. An emphasis on craft production to meet real social needs transmogrified into a never-never land inhabited by those who had grown rich on the immoral earnings of capitalism. Worpole cites one incident of this drama:

> Urban popular culture developed through commercial forms, and the crafts movement became associated with an Arcadian countryside or the sequestered lives of a privileged elite. Was there anything sadder in the history of English socialist remonstration than C.R. Ashbee's valediction for the Arts and Crafts Movement, when he wrote to Morris that, 'We have made of a great social movement a narrow and tiresome little aristocracy working with great skill for the very rich.'[66]

It is a theme to which we shall return briefly towards the end of this book.

The Madejski stadium and contemporary leisure may seem a curious introduction to a chapter about modern working practices. Yet the young man in the stadium shop is doing a 'real' job: so are the administrative staff, the public relations officer who arranged my visit to the stadium, the physiotherapists, the professional footballers and the staff of the Thames Valley Conference Centre which shares the facilities of the stadium; so are the three hundred and fifty caterers and stewards brought into the stadium on match days. Five hundred people were employed during the construction of the stadium, two hundred and fifty work there full-time and the hotel is likely to create another two hundred jobs.

---

66. Ken Worpole, 'Trading places: the city workshop', in *Whose cities?*, edited M. Fisher and U. Owen, (Penguin, 1991)

My first point, then, is that work has changed. Production expands, but actually employs fewer people as productivity increases; increasingly the jobs being created are in the 'service' sector — shops, banks and insurance firms, hotels and catering, transport, a range of professional services 'bought in' by larger firms from smaller ones. And of course what goes with this process is a change in the actual conditions of work. Increasing numbers of people work part-time, on temporary or fixed term contracts, or they are self-employed. Probably only about half the employable population of Western Europe are in 'typical' (i.e. full-time, permanent) jobs. Many of the 'new' jobs are taken by women. While it is true that women occupy an ever-increasing share of the labour market, the places they occupy are often still very different from (and in many ways inferior to) those occupied by men. On average, Reading women earn twenty percent less than men. If the exterior forms of power relationships between men and women have changed, there are obstinate deep inequalities which persist.

One way of assessing the changes taking place in the labour market is by looking at the life of the professional footballer. There is no doubt that they earn good money, even at Football League Second Division Reading. With pop stars, film actors, public relations executives, City traders and media people, footballers are part of the new aristocracy of labour. Yet these groups of workers produce nothing, if by production we mean material goods. Reading captain Phil Parkinson is nowhere near being a millionaire. Indeed, at thirty-one years old when I interviewed him in January 1999, Phil takes a very level-headed view of the world. He would be every mother's model son-in-law rather than a Hollywood heart-throb. He has played for Bury and Southampton, and Reading is probably as far as he is going as a player:

"I think when you're in your early twenties, you think 'this is great, all one big laugh really', but I'm thirty-one now and

I've got two kids, it's more like a business. You start thinking, right, I've this contract now, I've got eighteen months of my contract left, let's start planning, and you start planning financially because obviously football is a short career. You get paid well at the time, but if you play until you're thirty-five, you'll be very lucky. I think the top players in the Premiership, they're just businessmen now, I don't think they've got any deep love for the clubs they play for, they're just earning as much money as they can to invest for the future... At this club, if players look after their money, they're earning good money, but they're only on short-term contracts: they might be earning good money for two years, but it might be halved for the next contract."

Apart from being club captain he is also Reading representative for the Professional Footballers' Association (PFA). Largely through their work, footballers have a unique pension which matures at thirty-five, and the PFA urges players to put as much money as they can into their pensions. It advises young players "not to blow the money on stupid cars and things like that when they could be putting it into (their pension)".

At the same time, there is that overwhelming pleasure in doing well the one thing that you want to do more than anything else. It is a feeling which William Morris, the consummate craftsman, would have understood so well. Parkinson again:

"I think you'll find that most players who become footballers, it's the only thing they've ever wanted to do. It's been an ambition since they were very young. And that's the same with me — I (never) wanted to do anything else. I just had this one ambition to be a player."

Footballers need to be talented, they need to train hard, but they also need the mental hardness which comes from making a job out of the thing you most want to do in the world. In just the same way, as Morris's inheritance in Cornish mining shares declined in value, he too was forced to make of his design activities a business as well as a work of love and homage to the craft ideals of medieval England. Like many players, Phil Parkinson would like to stay in the game, as a coach and ultimately a manager, when his playing days are over. But he is hedging his bets. One rather unexpected and little known part of the work of the PFA is its support for education. It pays players under twenty-one all of the cost of any courses they want to do, going down to seventy percent thereafter but lasting throughout the member's life. Phil himself was in the third year of an Open University degree when I spoke to him, which has given him a new interest outside football, and one which may help him to develop an alternative career in the future.

William Morris and the morality of work

Personally, I have some doubts about whether 'a job for life' was ever quite such a good thing as it was made out to be. The day before I met Phil Parkinson, I had met a retired man of sixty, except that he wasn't retired because he had a pleasant four-hours a day job as caretaker at an adult education centre in a south coastal town. His parents had put his name down at birth to be a railway engine driver. After serving his apprenticeship and starting as a driver, he discovered that he wanted something more interesting than staring down the track looking for the next red signal. What parents want for their son or daughter may be very different from what the grown man or women wants. He has had a number of careers since, including management. But above all he likes people, working with people, being with people, making things happen between people. I cannot imagine him sitting at home alone, typing on a computer keyboard.

In the face of dissolving visions of work in our society, are Morris's views on the morality of work, deeply rooted in the Victorian tradition of Ruskin and Carlyle, completely out-of-date? As we get further from the particularities of Morris's life and the nature of the disputes about art, work and politics in which he was involved, so the deep structure of his beliefs has become increasingly plain and increasingly attractive. I want at this stage to bring in the words of Raymond Williams, from the Catalogue of the 1984 London ICA Morris exhibition. In an interview carried out in December 1982, Williams laid out the key features of Morris's approach to work. First of all he comments on the 'emphasis on meaning in work' (the words that preface this chapter). Secondly, he raises the issue of large-scale production requiring little creativity from the worker and questions to what extent future generations will seek identity and creativity in quite different aspects of their lives — unpaid work, such as DIY or caring, sport and leisure.

Thirdly, Williams argues for a renewed emphasis on 'growing, caring, tending' in harmony with natural resources and extends this to the caring sphere which he identifies as 'creativity with people rather than just with materials.' In an essay written at about the same time as the interview, called "'Industrial' and 'Post-Industrial' Society", Williams rails against the definition of skill in contemporary society, noting that:

> One of the first extraordinary effects of this is that, interacting as it does with the definition of work as employment, it relegates most of the fundamental forms of human work to the unskilled. All the ordinary nurture and care of people, and all ordinary homemaking and preparation of food, are in this lowest category or beneath it. Then, even within employment, the old skills of farming, gardening, fishing, lumbering are written down as unskilled.[67]

It is amusing to note here that William Morris fancied himself as both a cook and a fisherman, skills which are often now relegated to the sphere of 'leisure' rather than 'work'.

---

67. Raymond Williams, '"Industrial" and "post-industrial" society', in *Towards 2000* (Chatto and Windus, 1983) p.89

Skill, then, in industrial society, is defined in relation to machinery. Morris's attitude to machinery has been referred to often and almost as often misunderstood. He is frequently seen as having a single-minded commitment to craft work using hand tools rather than the machine production which had come to dominate Victorian England and had made it the 'workshop of the world.' Yet for Morris the crucial distinction is not between hand work and machine work, or even between skilled and unskilled work, but between what he describes as 'useful work' and 'useless toil'. This involves taking account of the purpose of the work, the conditions under which it is executed and the relations between those who own the means of production and those who work as wage-slaves. Such an approach allows Morris, in *How we live and how we might live* (1884), to take a larger and more humane view of the matter:

> I have spoken of machinery being used freely for releasing people from the more mechanical and repulsive part of necessary labour; and I know that to some cultivated people, people of the artistic turn of mind, machinery is particularly distasteful, and they will be apt to say you will never get your surroundings pleasant so long as you are surrounded by machinery. I don't quite admit that; it is the allowing machines to be our masters and not our servants that so injures the beauty of life nowadays. In other words, it is the token of the terrible crime we have fallen into of using our control of the powers of nature for the purpose of enslaving people, careless meantime of how much happiness we rob their lives of.
>
> Yet for the consolation of the artists I will say that I believe that a state of social order would probably lead at first to a great development of machinery for really useful purposes, because people will still be anxious about getting through the work necessary to holding society together; but that after a while they will find that there is not so much work to do as they expected, and that then they will have leisure to reconsider the whole subject; and if it seems to them that a certain

industry would be carried on more pleasantly as regards the worker, and more effectually as regards the goods, by using hand-work rather than machinery, they will certainly get rid of their machinery, because it will be possible for them to do so.

Thus Morris opens the way to use machines to reduce the 'toil' element of work but also recognises that within a society where production is for use rather than profit, there will be a gradual decline in production and therefore in the need for high levels of mechanisation. One of the most delightful features of *News from Nowhere* is the presentation of a world in which people regard hard manual labour, such as harvest, as a privilege and a joy, rather than as a chore. How much more useful to cut corn or build houses than to spend hours in a gym on exercise machines attempting to counteract the unhealthy impact of modern, sedentary life-styles! In an important letter to George Bainton, dated 6 May 1888, Morris wrote:

My belief is that the merely necessary labour, the labour that will supply us with food and shelter(,) will be a very light burden in the future, properly distributed as it will be; and that the greater part of the work we do will be done with pleasure, just as a poet writes a poem or an artist paints a picture: did I not say in a former letter that human happiness consisted in the pleasurable exercise of our energies?

I believe too that Morris's argument about mechanisation covers more recent arguments about information technology. For example, e-mail and faxes have clear practical value, but there is still much enjoyment to be had in crafting or receiving a well constructed letter. A CD ROM of William Morris's work is useful to recall or check a particular quotation on a particular subject but can never compete with the sensual pleasure of handling a richly ornate Kelmscott Press volume. As Fiona Mac-Carthy has commented: 'Morris has, uniquely, married

the tradition of socialism as a critique of political economy with the tradition of Romantic anti-industrialism.'

At this point the argument bifurcates. On the one hand,
Morris's arguments seem wholly relevant to a future society, and indeed aspects of his beliefs can be seen in the
practice of environmentalists, of artists and crafts-people,
and of those who have opted out of stressful financially-
oriented jobs into less stressful people-oriented jobs. They
also vindicate the vast contribution made to society which
is not formally classified as 'work': domestic tasks, caring
for children, older relatives and neighbours, the running
of the associations and clubs which characterise a busy
and effective civil society. Morris's arguments seem necessary ones if we are to move away from a society in which
talk of a 'sustainable economy' is a cliché mouthed by
those whose practice supports the present despoliation of
our world. Morris's arguments point us towards a world in
which national and ethnic rivalries can be defused by a
reconstruction of the world economy for the needs of people rather than the imperatives of profit. In general, we
already spend less hours on paid work than our Victorian
ancestors, or even our own parents. We retire earlier. Our
identity is increasingly tied up with our leisure activities
rather than our jobs.

Yet that is not the whole story. First of all, there is an
alternative critique of what is happening in the labour
market today which seems to look backwards regret-
fully to the days of 'jobs for life' rather than forwards to
a society in which work is reunited with other aspects of
human society (play, leisure, art). Richard Sennett, in a
book which was widely quoted in the insecure years of
the late 1990s, has linked the increasingly short-term
and at-a-distance working relationships of the modern
economy with the decline in family life and durable
social relationships. Sennett claims:

> It is the time dimension of the new capitalism, rather
> than hi-tech data transmission, global stock markets or

free trade, that most directly affects people's emotional lives outside the workplace.[68]

I rather doubt this. Sennett has picked on just one aspect of work organisation to stand for the whole. What is noticeable in Morris's life is how he conjoins deep commitment to people and ideals with a rather free-flowing lifestyle in which he moves from one new enthusiasm to another, from one realm of life to another. If at one level, human beings require an element of stability, they also need variety. One of my early jobs was in an engineering factory. It was often remarked on that one of the most distressing aspects of the firm was the number of men who having collected their fifty-year long service medal at aged sixty-five, were dead within a year or two. For stability, read dependency and an inability to develop a life outside of paid work.

The M4 Corridor: England's Silicon Valley

Rather more worrying is the way in which aspects of the labour market seem to be going in quite a different direction from those I have suggested above. It is also a direction of central interest to those who live and work in and around Reading. In what now seem the halcyon years between 1950 and 1975, years of full employment and rising real wages, working hours declined steadily. Saturday morning working became a thing of the past for most factory and office workers. In exchange, workers delivered to their employers some modest gains in productivity. Inefficiencies were masked by high rates of growth throughout Western Europe and the United States of America. But in the aftermath of the profound crisis produced by the 1973 increases in the cost of oil, employers began to look again

68. Richard Sennett, *The Corrosion of character: the personal consequences of work in the new capitalism*, (Norton, 1998)

at how productivity gains might be ratcheted up, using the availability of cheap labour sources in the developing countries as a stick with which to beat the back of workers in the industrial world.

Economics is a very inexact science, indeed some commentators would describe it as closer to black magic than science. Much of it depends on common sense. It is obvious, I think, that because profit in capitalist enterprises derives from the simple fact that workers' labour is worth more than they get paid for it, then if more work can be squeezed out of workers for the same pay, it follows that profitability will improve. This particular piece of economic sleight of hand has become the central pillar of American business practice and perhaps explains why the USA has been rather more successful than other countries at increasing employment in the years since 1990. On the one hand there is the soft rhetoric of 'flexibility', 'portfolio careers' and quality control. On the other hand is the harsh reality of neoliberalism: job intensification, longer hours, higher output targets, hire-and-fire and unpaid overtime. Neither are these processes confined to the private sector, as Dinah Livingstone, in her splendid prose and verse anthology *Work*, makes clear:

> Full-time workers now work much longer hours. In addition, many workers, such as doctors, nurses and teachers have an enormously increased load of paperwork, much of it directly related to the fact that their institution has now become a 'trust', 'fundholder' or 'corporation'. This is exhausting and makes it much harder to do their real job of looking after their patients or students properly. Neoliberalism favours 'flexibilisation' and 'casualisation'. In the 1970s women fought for more flexible hours so that they could combine jobs with, for example, picking up children from school. 'Flexibilisation' today means the opposite. It is the worker who has to be 'flexible' not the boss. Shop workers, who work long hours for low pay, are now required to be 'flexible' enough to work late at night, even all night, and on Sundays.[69]

---

69. *Work*, pages 292-3

The frequent use of inverted commas in this quotation is significant, since it is through language and the manipulation of language that a particular and partial view of the world is presented as the only future possible. If utopia means anything, it means the right to define our own future. Part of the purpose of this book is to reclaim the hard-edged meanings of liberty, equality and community from those who wish to subvert them for their own selfish ends.

So what of Reading? Reading is central to this argument not just because it shares with the rest of the country a number of features we have inherited from the dark night of Tory rule from 1979-97. It is precisely in this part of England that we find the highest concentration of high tech firms in the country. Many of them are American. It is precisely those industries at the forefront of the information revolution that should be uncoiling human beings from the manacles of useless toil. Yet it is precisely those same firms which are at the forefront of this new drive for ever-greater levels of profitability at the expense of their own workforces.

While bigger than Slough, Reading seems to suffer from the same sense of itself as a rather provisional place. Where the city centre should be, there is a messy public space between the 'new' Civic Centre, Police and Magistrates Court and Broad Street shopping mall and car-park. I wondered whether Reading was happier with the private than the public, or whether perhaps the public is just a more uphill struggle. In this space there are drinkers, a few surprisingly good and cheap market-stalls with shoppers of a variety of ethnic backgrounds. There is a memorial to three local men who died in the Spanish Civil war, sculpted in stone by Eric Stanford, Keeper of Art at Reading Museum, who was given a year off by Reading Borough Council to accomplish the task.[70] Even the entrance to the Civic Centre

---

70. C. Williams et al, *Memorials of the Spanish Civil War* (Sutton Publishing, 1996), p.110

is messy — the most visible sign is the one which says 'Post Office', which just happens to be inside. But there is good practical stuff here too — such as the short-stay creche for people visiting the Civic Centre on Council business, the sign advertising 'free checks for prams and pushchairs' in the Mall. In Reading the fact that things 'work' seems to matter more than their appearance.

Reading is a growth town. Between 1988 and 1997 it gained twenty-eight thousand jobs and two hundred and sixty-three firms. An official report stated that the area

> possesses a skilled and well qualified workforce, enjoys a high quality of life, has good transport links, has or is near a number of the UK's leading academic and research establishments. During the last few years, Thames Valley has successfully become a major focus for overseas investment, particularly in the IT, electronics and telecommunications sectors.[71]

Half the firms in the area say their market is global, rather than local, regional or national. Reading is still a commuter base for people travelling up to London to work, but it is also a commuter destination in its own right, with many thousands travelling in and out each day.

There is something almost mythical about Reading and work, no doubt because it has managed to avoid much of the slaughter of British industry which took place in the early and mid-1980s. A group of local academics published a book in 1987 called *Western Sunrise* in which they managed the very clever feat of both challenging the more inflated notions of an English Silicon Valley stretching west down the M4 from London, while at the same time feeding on and contributing to that very myth. Even in 1987 they could report that 'Most of the large companies now represented in the area are overseas and particularly

---

71. *Thames valley: economic and labour market trends 1997* (Reading, Thames Valley Enterprise)

American companies'.[72] The factors of chief importance in this growth were seen as the birth of smaller high tech firms as spin-offs of larger firms, access to Heathrow airport and the supply of qualified labour.

More controversially and less obviously, the authors go on to outline in some detail and stress the importance of the existence of government research establishments (GREs) in the area such as the Atomic Weapons Research Establishment at Aldermaston, the Royal Aircraft Establishment at Farnborough and the Atomic Energy Research Establishment at Harwell. The authors of *Western Sunrise* show how the GREs acquired considerable importance during the Second World War and afterwards during the Cold War. While the nature of the GREs forms the basis for some of the argument in the next chapter about Abingdon and risk, the most important point for our present concern is that 'They began to develop close contractual relationships with high tech industries — especially in electronics production.' The authors record how

> ...after 1945, with the rapid development of a military-industrial complex in Britain, they quickly came to form the nodes of an intricate web of defence procurement, in which close and intimate contacts between research establishments and high tech contractors became the everyday rule.[73]

They point out that although there is a tendering process, part of the government's role is to select and cultivate likely firms. In 1983/84, at the height of concern about American Cruise missiles coming to nearby Greenham Common, and a trigger-happy US President Reagan, the equipment budget of the Ministry of Defence was £7,800 million, forty-six percent of total defence budget, plus £700 million on R&D and 'management'.

---

72. P. Hall et al, *Western sunrise: the genesis and growth of Britain's major high tech corridor* (Allen and Unwin, 1987) p.176
73. *Western sunrise*, p.121

The Ministry was the biggest customer of UK industry and fifty percent of R&D was channelled through it.

If the background to the Reading miracle is less than appetising, the reality of working for one of these high tech United States firms is equally alarming. Jonathan Brunert made a film called 'Workaholics' for BBC TV's Panorama programme, shown in September 1998. The programme stated its case very simply in the headline-catching first sentence: 'More and more people are working long hours'. This was seen as another North American import, 'the Americanisation of working culture'. The example quoted at some length in the film was Oracle, the second largest computer software firm in the UK, which employed four thousand, five hundred in the UK at the time the film was made, many of them in steel and glass offices in Reading.

Like so many television documentaries, 'Workaholics' was inconclusive. Alongside some horror stories about the impact of long hours on family life and personal health, figures were quoted from a survey of one thousand employees working more than forty-eight hours per week which showed that seventy-two percent enjoy work and don't mind the hours. Even the assumed link between long hours and divorce does not hold good, with the strains of long hours more than compensated for by the financial advantages. The Oracle employee featured in the film trades long hours for large bonuses, an idealised rural life-style and the latest in high tech consumer goods. 'Workaholics' suggested, without any very specific evidence, that the worst impact of long hours may be on women, since even professional women tend to be more involved in domestic work and childcare than men. For too many women it is still a case of 'career versus family', with experiments designed to balance working life and home life such as job-sharing still regarded as marginal to the labour market. While the European Working Time directive may have some impact on working hours in England, it will not tackle the problem that many workers feel they have to put in extra voluntary

138

hours or agree to work overtime, in order to protect their jobs. Morris's arguments about work as a moral good as well as a practical necessity, remain largely ignored. Work brings in money, regardless of its intrinsic value.

Reading, Robinson and Routemasters

William Morris saw Victorian England as an age of makeshift. He was a frequent visitor to Charles Rowley's Ancoats Brotherhood in Manchester. 'Makeshift' was the subject of his last talk there in 1894, just two years before his death.[74] In characterising Victorian England as the age of makeshift, he contrasted previous ages which would be remembered as the Age of Learning or Age of Chivalry. And makeshift went through society, including housing, food, education and leisure. One version of the history of the twentieth century is the record of the defeat of public attempts to place English culture (what Raymond Williams described as culture-as-a-way-of-life) on a firmer foundation than would be strictly allowed for by the practice of laissez-faire economics, what would nowadays be called 'the market'. Thus 'homes fit for heroes' in the years after the First World War, in contrast to the antisocial tower-blocks of the 1960s, the healthy diet achieved in England during the Second World War compared with the sugar- and additive-stuffed food of more recent decades, the struggle for a humane and comprehensive public education system compared with the current obsessive interest in test results (if you can't measure it, it's not worth even trying to do it).

One of the more surprising features of Reading is seeing the old familiar red London buses, the vintage Routemasters with the open platform at the back, coming round the corner. The council has set up a workshop to keep these

---

74. See also Edmund and Ruth Frow, *William Morris in Manchester and Salford* (Working Class Movement Library, 1996)

buses in service by recycling parts from one bus to another, which effectively often means turning two broken down vehicles into one serviceable bus. Robinson noticed the Routemasters near the beginning of Patrick Keiller's film 'Robinson in Space' in the spring of 1995. They are, after all, extremely big and very red. He notes also apparently random facts such as the employment of the French poet Rimbaud as teacher of French here in 1874, Jane Austen being educated in two rooms above Abbey gateway, next door to Reading Jail where Oscar Wilde was imprisoned. 'The true mystery of the world is the visible, not the invisible', the commentary informs us, quoting Wilde. I am struck here by the observations of George Sturt in *The Wheelwright's Shop* not so far away in Farnham in Surrey. Sturt notes the very change that Morris was both annotating and reacting against: the transition from traditional craft-based to new factory-based industries. He writes that

> Village life was dying out; intelligent interest in the country-side was being lost; the class war was disturbing erstwhile quiet communities; yet nobody saw what was happening. What we saw was some apparently trivial thing, such as the incoming of tin pails instead of wooden buckets.[75]

We have now seen plastic buckets replace tin pails. Using our eyes is one simple tool for understanding the present and maybe beginning to influence the shape of the future.

What, then, should we understand when we see an old red bus on the streets of Reading? The key to this is the management push to replace the old-style buses with a driver and conductor by new style driver-only buses. The economic arguments are compelling: a fifty percent reduction in staffing costs means buses can be run as profitable private concerns. Yet the old 'inefficient' Routemaster is

---

75. George Sturt, The wheelwright's shop (1923), Cambridge University Press Canto edition, 1993, p.154

actually faster around any given town than the new-style buses, with their interminable waits at bus-stops while the driver takes the fares. If buses are faster, use will increase, more fares will be collected, the environment will be less polluted and there will be less cars on the road. That is another way to define efficiency. Surveys of business firms in the Reading area are contradictory in defining the motorway network as a very positive factor, and the traffic congestion as a negative factor. As in so many aspects of our lives, we need a new economics and a new accounting.

Despite the local success of Reading in generating jobs, there is no evidence at all that such jobs will be in the manufacturing industries. Looking at the position nationally, jobs can be created, but they will be in service industries. This includes services such as public transport, hospitals, schools and community care, which were never meant to run at a profit. Even in the Thames Valley, more of the high tech firms are service industries than are producing objects. There is also a significant body of evidence now available that 'going for green' is one way of creating jobs. The buses in Reading are just one example of this. In chapter nine I shall suggest that less intensive agricultural methods are another way of creating jobs. Environmental control is yet a third. It is absurd to suggest we cannot afford this. The negative costs to the country of the Common Agricultural Policy, or cleaning up the pollution of both past and present generations, is enormous. It is perfectly possible to both compete in high tech global markets, and to make national and local decisions which both create jobs and deal more sympathetically with our natural environment. At some stage it takes political will. But it is clear from the large number of local initiatives taking place that people and voluntary organisations are not prepared to wait.

One such initiative is the existence in Reading of two LETS schemes. LETS stands for Local Exchange Trading Scheme and aims to promote the 'real economy' of deprived communities by encouraging people to trade in skills and services, using a local currency In one case, these are 'Kennets' from the name of the tributary of the Thames which joins it hereabouts; in the other case 'Readies'; exactly what these people lack. So far, I have referred to Reading as a particularly affluent town, yet as so often this gloss masks pockets of real deprivation. According to staff at Reading Borough Council, one fifth of the population live in the worst ten percent of wards in the country, measuring this across factors such as unemployment, lack of skills, benefit dependency and housing conditions. In one small area, twenty-five percent are unskilled compared to a Reading average of five percent. Unemployment has fallen, yet the number of long-term unemployed remains constant. And as in so many other communities, unemployment is a particular problem for black and Asian people in the town. One of the LETS schemes, which receives support from the Borough Council, makes a particular point of involving voluntary groups, such as women's groups and ethnic minority groups.

Other developments being encouraged by the Borough Council in what is often called the 'third sector economy' include a Credit Union and Community Businesses. Credit Unions are targeted at people who find it difficult to access credit in more conventional ways. Government support for them, as part of its overall plans to counter social exclusion, are likely to make them commoner and more effective in the future. It is ironical that at a time when the mutual principle is under threat in other parts of national life, most noticeably in the scandal of the conversion of building societies into limited company banks, mutuality is once again flourishing at the local community level, where it began. Community Businesses under discussion in Reading in 1999 included a group of Muslim women who had completed a Women in Business course funded by the European Social Fund and now wanted to put their learning into action. In similar fashion, a group of young men wanted to move on from the government's New Deal scheme for the unemployed to set up a grounds maintenance business. In both cases, profits would be recycled locally rather than being taken out of deprived communities, as happens with many conventional firms.

I have made a number of diffuse arguments in this book about work in capitalist society. Firstly, that capitalism, with the ethical hole in its heart, is not only an evil, but a stricken beast. Secondly that the battle against global capitalism is not waged at an international or corporate level, and is no longer waged at a class level. Thirdly, that the priorities identified by Morris — equality, human values before machine values, a certain harmony between people and the environment they inhabit, creativity and happiness before profit — still stand. Present ways of living and working produce disorganisation and conflict. But the ways of achieving those preferred objectives are the sum total of a thousand and one solutions being worked out by people in a wide variety of contexts to develop solidaristic and humane and orderly responses. If the problem is global, the solutions are local. For the moment, at least.

Morris's view that capitalism cannot be tamed, only overthrown, and that any other approach was a diversion from the 'real task', is no longer tenable. People have to function at the level that seems real to them, where they think they may be able to produce small, local changes, even if they have no picture of what the sum of their small, local solutions might look like.

Chapter 7
Abingdon and Risk

It is reported that sailors who fell into the Thames in the early nineteenth century did not drown, but rather choked to death inhaling the foul-smelling and poisonous fumes of the London sewer... It is nevertheless striking that hazards in those days assaulted the nose or the eyes and were thus perceptible to the senses, while the risks of civilisation today typically escape perception and are localised in the sphere of physical and chemical formulas (e.g. toxins in foodstuffs or the nuclear threat). (Ulrich Beck)[76]

Less lucky than King Midas, our green fields and clear waters, nay, the very air we breathe, are turned not to gold (which might please some of us for an hour maybe) but to dirt; and to speak plainly we know full well that under the present gospel of Capital not only there is no hope of bettering it, but that things grow worse year by year, day by day. Let us eat and drink, for to-morrow we die, choked by filth. (William Morris, *Art and the People*, 1884)

On the nature of risk

Ulrich Beck and Anthony Giddens are towering figures in the pitifully small world of social observation and comment. Anthony Giddens has defined more clearly than anyone the dilemmas of modern life.[77] On the one hand, the possibility of society, of life together in communities, depends on trust. On the other hand, we face a world of increasing uncertainty in which individual people feel vulnerable and at risk. We trust no-one, but we must trust

---

76. Ulrich Beck, *Risk society: towards a new modernity* (1986), translated by Mark Ritter (Sage, 1992)
77. Anthony Giddens, *The consequences of modernity* (Polity Press, 1990) and *Modernity and self-identity* (Polity Press, 1991).

everyone. A few years previously, Ulrich Beck had developed his concept of Risk Society, a phrase which only became common currency in English with the publication of an English translation in 1992.[78] Beck's thesis was that the logic of industrial society, of disciplined units of industrial production, had been overtaken by the logic of risk production: 'At the centre lie the risks and consequences of modernisation, which are revealed as irreversible threats to the life of plants, animals and human beings.'[79] Where pollution from a factory affects chiefly those living near the factory, risks such as nuclear accidents and global warming have a global impact. Small Pacific island nations, which contribute little or nothing to global warming, may disappear altogether as ice-caps and glaciers melt and sea levels rise.

But risks are experienced by people who live specific lives in specific locations. People in Oxfordshire worry about radiation from the atomic power research station at Harwell, just as the concerns of people about nuclear warfare were often related to their local air force base where nuclear bombers or cruise missiles were based. The fundamental point about risk is that it is not an abstract, theoretical, text-book debate but something which is experienced by real people within the communities in which they live. In December 1998, just a few days before Christmas, the United States and British governments effectively declared war on Iraq by launching missiles against anti-aircraft installations in Iraq. The objective was to clear the way for further bomber and missile attacks on facilities at which is was claimed that Sadam Hussein was developing a capability to manufacture and 'deliver' (i.e. use) nuclear, chemical and biological weapons. That morning, the newspapers were full of the story and the coincidence of its timing with an important House of Representatives vote on the possible impeach-

78. Ulrich Beck, *Risk society*, p.21
79. Ulrich Beck, *Risk society*, p.13

ment of President Clinton for lying about his sexual activities in the White House. Hidden away on page seven of the *Guardian* on 18 December were two stories which remind us that risk comes as often as not from sources closer to home than the evil intentions of foreign dictators.

Atom plants told to act on safety or risk disaster

This commented on a report by the nuclear inspectorate, due to be published in January 1999, but already in the House of Lords library. Quite apart from the risks of unstable materials stored at the British Nuclear Fuels (BNFL) plant at Sellafield in Cumbria, the report suggests that: 'All eight old Magnox nuclear stations need remedial work along with the nuclear weapons plant at Aldermaston in Berkshire and the UK Atomic Energy Authority site at Harwell in Oxfordshire.' Specific mention was made of 'radioactive sludge at Aldermaston' with the potential for leaking.

Major ignored BSE warnings

This was a report of the public enquiry into BSE (mad cow disease), which was taking place in London. Douglas Hogg had been giving evidence which suggested that he argued in Cabinet for a much stronger line than was actually taken at the time of the 1996 BSE crisis. In particular, he argued for a ban on all cattle over the age of thirty months entering the food chain, a policy which he suggested might have avoided the subsequent costly ban on all beef exports, which was still in place two and a half years later. A minute of one Cabinet meeting reveals that Prime Minister John Major's view was that 'the risk of contracting CJD was considerably less than the risks of contracting lung cancer, for example, but the government had not only failed to ban smoking, it had failed to ban even the advertising of smoking.' Hogg said that he either had to accept his colleagues' views or resign, and of course resigning was not an option which members of the Major government accepted with any great enthusiasm.

On risk in the Thames valley

In the previous chapter, we saw how the high tech industries which dominate the Reading area, have a close relationship to the circle of research establishments in the Thames valley between Reading and Oxford. Government contracts fuelled the fortunes of many firms, skilled workforces were developed and new industries took root. Often the products and services of these firms bear little connection with the Cold War-related projects and products which fathered them.

Abingdon, a quiet little market town turned commuter town on the Thames as it heads north for Oxford, lies at the epicentre of this circle of government research centres. My initial visit in October 1997 was reassuring, although as I drove across the downs on the A34 road, I was conscious of the smoke of the tall chimneys of Didcot power station drifting over the stubble fields even before I saw the bulk of the plant itself. Idly I wondered whether it or Windsor castle might be the largest building in the Thames Valley. 'Robinson', you might say, was here, with Paul Scofield, the unseen voice of the narrator, observing in his clipped manner that five percent of the peak demand for electricity in England comes from this one power station. He observed that a second gas-fired power station was being built here, as part of the government's 'dash for gas'. This would allow the government to close down most of what remained of the coal industry and thereby ensure that the miners would never again be a threat to the government, one of the ideas that runs through Patrick Keiller's film 'Robinson in Space'. It would also, of course, make it easier for Britain to meet its international commitments about emissions, while making nonsense of energy policy by losing energy efficiency as one energy source (gas) is converted into another (electricity).

On the other side of the A34 I could see 'secret' Harwell, surrounded by trees, oddly shaped towers peeping above them — the perfect way, I thought, to advertise a well-kept secret.

Abingdon has a 60s shopping mall which is 'disapproved of'. It is easy to see why, since it is common and ordinary in a town that prides itself on being extraordinary. People are prouder of their Charter Centre, a more recent complex of public buildings which includes a Citizens Advice Bureau, social services, a library and an Old People's Day Centre. If there is 'no such thing as society', Margaret Thatcher clearly forgot to inform the thirty-four thousand inhabitants of Abingdon. In the library, I am offered the Oxfordshire County Council community groups A-Z, as well as the Abingdon Who's Who and Directory which lists all residents in alphabetical order and by streets. I notice too that the list of councillors doesn't mention political parties for either town council or district council. Abingdon elected a Liberal Democrat MP in 1997, rather to its surprise.

Abingdon tries hard to be a European town with twinning arrangements with a whole raft of European cities — Argentan and Colmar in France, Lucca in Italy, Schongau in Germany and Saint Niklaus in Belgium. In the Council offices, the European Union flag is flying in the reception area. The receptionist agrees that European twinning activities are important, although they do have one man who regularly complains about 'that flag.' Even the Job Centre carries glad tidings — a wide range of relatively well paid full-time jobs, and rates for part-time work which would have surprised (in those pre-minimum wage days) the inhabitants of Birmingham or Cornwall. I sit in the church of St Nicholas writing up my notes: that particular feel of a small English town where all the shops shut at exactly five; people going home by car and bike — the influence of Oxford, already, I wondered? I am interrupted by the vicar, a mild, slightly distant man of about sixty. He too wants to shut up shop. The river is a short walk down Bridge Street from the Market Square. There is an island with a pub, the Mill House, and from the Mill House garden, a quiet view of still dark green water, swans and back on the town side of the river, a hotel called the Upper Reaches. London seems a long way away.

St Helen's, Abingdon's parish church, is a splendid waterfront church that has become almost square with much building of side aisles. It has the distinction of being the second-widest church in England. Its handsome spire rising at the river's edge offers a foretaste of the 'dreaming spires' of Oxford itself and the pretty spire of Lechlade reflected in the willow-margined stream of the upper reaches of the Thames, beyond Kelmscott. There are almshouses too for the elderly and infirm, to support them in the predictable risks of old age. The one apparent note of discord is an article from the Times pinned on the church notice-board about an outbreak of sleeping sickness in Lucca, Abingdon's twin town. Could this be why the town centre was emptying so rapidly of people by six o'clock in the evening? 'To bed to bed, says sleepy head'. Then just as I am about to give up on Abingdon as being too impossibly nice, I come across the Frugal Food shop with a group of artistic-looking people celebrating a book launch by Nigel Bray, local author, now resident in Oxford. His novel[80] is set in the area and is, he says, about the 'insecurities and fears of modern man'. So what are the insecurities and fears lurking behind the smooth façade of Abingdon, and how and when do they come from the surface, I wonder. When I eventually got round to reading the novel, I found a hot-potch of ideas, a lot of humour, some of it feeble, much of it darkly black, and some inventive typography. But above all it is an angry book, angry about unemployment and poverty and the insecurities that are imposed on us from outside as well as the ones welling up within our own souls. Rafael, the protagonist, keeps what he calls an Index of Unrealities: it

---

80. Nigel Bray, *Millennium haul* (Gambara Press, 1997)

will come as no surprise to those weary of the twentieth century to find that TRUTH, thus, in capital letters, is 'of course' one of the entries.

On nuclear war and nuclear peace

George and Vi Colliety are old friends from London who moved to Abingdon a number of years ago to be closer to their married daughter and grandchildren. We became friends the morning after the 1987 hurricane. George lived at the end of our street, and the wind tearing up from the North Downs hit his gardens especially badly. My son and I helped him to clear the wreckage of his greenhouse and tidy up a pile of bricks that had once been a garden wall. Vi and George were part of our 'London village'.

His father had been a trade unionist and a Labour Party member, and George has followed in his footsteps. Both George and Vi were happy that the war had ended when the cities of Hiroshima and Nagasaki ceased to exist beneath giant mushroom clouds in 1945, but George is sure in retrospect that these explosions only hastened a victory which by then was inevitable.

George: "It wasn't necessary — I think peace would have come. It may have taken a little bit longer, but by that time the Japanese had had enough."

Vi: "Mind you, at the time we were all very happy!"

There was shock and horror at the photos of the devastated cities, but only gradually did it dawn on the minds of people in general that this was a new sort of weapon, a new sort of technology. And it was only as people took sick and died from radiation poisoning years later, as babies were born crippled and deformed, that it emerged that these new weapons not only destroyed the present but mortgaged the future in a new and terrifying way. On a visit to Japan in

1983, Tony Benn met some of the survivors of the bomb blasts at Hiroshima and Nagasaki, the Hibakusha. Three hundred and seventy thousand of them were still alive, but of those who had died, cancer was the cause of two thirds of the deaths.[81] George became involved in Teachers for Peace right at the start of his teaching career in the 1950s. Some of those he worked with were Communist Party members, which in the context of the Cold War gave rise to the accusation that this group were more interested in supporting Mother Russia than in peace. As George put it:

> "A lot of the people involved were Communist Party members, but because they were Communist Party members, instead of listening to what they were saying, it was more or less 'Oh, you're just spouting the party line'."

With the arrival on the scene of the Campaign for Nuclear Disarmament (CND), Teachers for Peace became the Teachers Campaign for Nuclear Disarmament, with George as its national secretary. There was much criticism of involvement of teachers in the peace movement. George was 'named' as a CP member (although he wasn't), one of a group who were indoctrinating the children under their care. Someone suggested they should sue but, as George said, "you couldn't, there was nothing you could do about it, you just had to take it. To sue you had to have a lot of money, and you had no backing, so you just had to accept it... This is the sort of pressure people were under at that time."

It was, of course, the age of the McCarthy witch-hunts in the United States of America.

The Aldermaston marches are nowadays remembered as being from the Nuclear Weapons Research Establishment at Aldermaston to Trafalgar Square in London. Few remember that the first march was to Aldermaston — from London. The marchers set off in the rain:

---

81. Tony Benn, *The end of an era: diaries 1980-90,* edited Ruth Winstone, (Century, 1992) p.313

"I'm quite sure the powers-that-be wanted it to fail, they wanted it to be a miserable failure. There wasn't a lot of people on that march, on that first day, and it poured with rain, it was dreadful, but we had the photographs, the film, of these people who were determined to do this, and on the second day, many, many more people came out."

Even after all these years, George remembers with some bitterness both the personal cost and the behaviour of the police, whose job should be to protect democracy. He remembers one lobby of Parliament when in order to silence some singing in the lobby queue outside the Houses of Parliament (Morris's dung-hill, let us remember), mounted police charged the queue, determined to scatter everyone:

"I got home and we turned the 9 o'clock news on, on the radio, and the newsperson said 'The demonstration was peaceful until the arrival of the mounted police.' I was astonished hearing that, so I immediately rang (my friend) and said 'Bert, listen to the ten o'clock news, it's absolutely surprising.' Ten o'clock news — nothing — it had been cut... Those mounted police actually chased people from Parliament Square and they took them, chased them, way up past Euston. It was that sort of attitude from the hierarchy and the people in authority."

I was struck transcribing the tape of our discussion some months later by the similarity of Morris's description of the Bloody Sunday riot of November 13th 1887, when police attacked a demonstration of the unemployed and their political supporters, which Fiona MacCarthy describes as 'the most ruthless display of establishment power that London has ever seen.'[82] When he came to write about this episode in chapter seven of *News from Nowhere*, Morris treats it in an ironical dialogue between Guest (the Morris character) and Dick, his guide to *Nowhere*. But the anger shines through:

---

82. Fiona MacCarthy, *William Morris*, p.567

"Well," quoth I, "but after all your Mr. James is right so far, and it is true; except that there was no fighting, merely unarmed and peaceable people attacked by ruffians armed with bludgeons."

"And they put up with that?" said Dick, with the first unpleasant expression I had seen on his good-tempered face.

Said I, reddening: "We had to put up with it; we couldn't help it."

The old man looked at me keenly, and said: "You seem to know a great deal about it, neighbour! And is it really true that nothing came of it?"

"This came of it," said I, "that a good many people were sent to prison because of it."

"What, of the bludgeoners?" said the old man. "Poor devils!"

"No, no," said I, "of the bludgeoned."

Said the old man rather severely: "Friend, I expect that you have been reading some rotten collection of lies, and have been taken in by it too easily."

In later years it became obvious to George and his friends that the large number of United States nuclear bases in Britain made it little more than "an American bomb-carrier". With the arrival of cruise missiles in the 1980s this suspicion was confirmed, strengthened by the new militancy of the feminist movement, with their peace camps at places such as Greenham Common. Vi commented how frightened and worried people were in those days, whereas nowadays they seem largely unconcerned. George pointed out that small peace groups still exist round the country, including one in Abingdon, though their remit is rather broader than just nuclear weapons. Certainly the threat remains, in the form of lethal weapons treated as boyish toys, increasingly out of political control. In retrospect, the original CND slogan of 'Ban the Bomb' now seems hopelessly naïve. Beyond the problem of a nation deciding it does not need such weapons, there is the next problem of how to physically dispose of the weapons, and beyond that the problem of how human kind can somehow ''forget' the knowledge of how to make the weapons.

We went on to discuss the issue of so-called 'peaceful' nuclear power, and here George felt that everybody had been misled:

"The publicity was that that this was a new form of power, it's going to be cheap, it's going to be clean, the spent fuel can be sent for reprocessing and used again, and so on. It's now shown quite clearly that this was all false."

Tony Benn has demonstrated in his *Diaries* that even Government ministers were not fully informed of all the risks which the scientists knew about. He makes two claims in particular. Firstly that nuclear power was forty percent more expensive than was claimed and three times the cost of coal.[83] On that reckoning, of course, it would have been possible to fit proper emission controls on coal-fired power stations and still produce energy more cheaply than by nuclear power. Secondly, that plutonium from civil power stations was supplied to the United States of America:

From 1966 to 1970 and from 1975 to 1979 I was the Minister responsible for atomic energy, and I had absolutely no knowledge of this. Encouraged by my officials, I used to give talks on the use of civil nuclear power, while all the time our civil power stations were supplying plutonium for American nuclear weapons.[84]

I followed up these issues with Jean Saunders, formerly active in Oxfordshire Friends of the Earth. Like most successful campaigning groups, Friends of the Earth has a simple position, summed up in the slogan 'Think globally, act locally'. If the public image of environmental campaigners is of rather pedantic, solemn spoil-sports, they should meet Jean — a happy, cheerful person, dressed in

83. Tony Benn, *The end of an era*, p.563
84. Tony Benn, *The end of an era*, p.312

bright clothes, with a big garden full of trees and flowers in a village between Faringdon and Swindon. Jean's affinity with Morris is long-standing. She worked with the project which eventually gave rise to a William Morris Society publication about rural issues, edited by the late John Kay.[85] Jean wrote the chapter in the book on the green agenda for agriculture. We had both read an article by Chris Busby in which he picked up on a cluster of leukaemia cases around Harwell.[86] He claims that radioactive waste from Harwell was released as gases into the air, via a sewer into a local stream, and via a pipeline into the Thames at Sutton Courtenay. But pursuing this is hard work, as Jean explained:

> "There has been this cluster of leukaemia cases which Chris Busby was picking up on and raising concern about, but they just dismiss it again, and say we're just scare-mongering — you get accused of scare-mongering all the time when you're an environmental activist!"

While it was easy to persuade journalists to write about radiation from the weapons establishment at Aldermaston, it was much harder to get them to write about pollution from the 'peaceful' reactors at Harwell. The image of 'research' remains that of a bland, neutral activity. Concern at Harwell in the 1980s centred on a number of issues. The nuclear reactors themselves were coming to the end of their useful life. There was an incinerator burning radioactive waste. The Thames was being used for waste disposal. There was storage of drums originally intended for dumping at sea but stranded after a decision to ban that. The geology of Harwell, on the chalk downs, is an important part of the story. All ground-water goes

---

85. (edited) John Kay, *'News from nowhere' and the English country-side: a centenary celebration placed in the landscape, buildings and people of West Oxfordshire and the neighbouring counties* (William Morris Society, 1990)

86. Chris Busby, 'The Thames valley — a radioactive breeding ground for cancer', *The Ecologist*, volume 27, No.5, October 1997

straight down through the chalk and emerges in the springline villages. There was ground-water contamination not just from radioactive waste but also from solvents. As a result, the romantically named village of Blewbury on the A417 Wantage-Reading road, south of Didcot, lost its water supply. The risks, unlike Morris's dirt, may be invisible, but they are present and have impacted on the lives of local people.

Harwell is now a dumping ground, and Jean and her friends have worked hard to ensure that it is a relatively safe one:

> "At the moment it's being used very much as a waste store. Millions of pounds have been spent on building an intermediate radioactive waste store at Harwell which has only just come on stream last year... Our worry in Oxfordshire has always been because of the concern about radioactive waste and the concerns to do with the disposal of waste underground which was never really a viable proposal." (With the failure of NIREX to get planning permission for a facility at Sellafield, Harwell seems to have become a repository for radioactive waste.) "What we are concerned about is that because Harwell has been covered by what's called a special development order, they've done everything without planning permission... which meant they didn't have any environmental impact assessment carried out either."

She sees this as denial of proper democratic participation through planning regulations. A further concern is the development of the business park with factories, offices and four hundred houses, next to a site that is radioactive and still leaking solvents.

On the food we eat

Both conversations, separated by a period of three months in 1999, led on to the issue of genetically modified crops. Just as supporters of nuclear power argue that it is a 'clean' way to produce energy, so supporters of genetic modification argue that this new way of breeding crops will produce more food more efficiently. George saw both views as tunnel vision, ignoring the unknown future risks involved:

"I think what you have here is a very narrow presentation because they are saying that you will not need all these pesticides, you will be able to get greater yields, we'll then be able to feed the world, and so on and so forth, the usual arguments... but then they don't look outside that and the effect on the environment outside of what they are doing, the effect upon wildlife, that's not taken into account, it's just a narrow tunnel these people look down, and the tunnel is one where they're looking for profit".

This view is not just that of CND veterans and environmental activists. In committing itself to exclude GM ingredients from its 'own brand' products, the freezer store group Iceland put the interests of the US-based multinational Monsanto very firmly at the top of the GM agenda:

Soya beans are grown mainly in North America and find their way into sixty percent of all processed foods. For example, they are in bread, biscuits, baby foods, chocolate, ice cream, ready meals and many vegetarian products. Monsanto, the giant chemical factory, has modified a soya bean with genetic material from a virus and a petunia linked to a bacterial gene, which has made the soya plant resistant to a weedkiller called Roundup, which is also manufactured by Monsanto.[87]

While much of Jean's work has been concerned with the nuclear risk, Friends of the Earth is very much involved with the genetic modification issue. By coincidence, she lives very close to Lushill Farm, near Swindon, where the first farm-scale trial of GM oilseed rape took place in 1999. It got off to a bad start with a failure to advertise properly

87. Iceland Frozen Foods plc leaflet, 1998

to the locals that the trial was taking place, and things went downhill rapidly.

Rather to her surprise, Jean found the locals as concerned as outsiders about the trial, in contrast to her experience of nuclear power:

"In a lot of ways, it's been easier (to oppose GM crops). In the nuclear industry... you also tended to find that your local communities worked in the power stations, and so it was their bread and butter, and so it was quite difficult to raise local opposition to the nuclear industry because they were directly involved... The farmer next door to the fields where the crops are being grown was probably more angry about the whole thing than anyone else. He said his wife had to restrain him from going and getting the tractor and digging it up himself. He was so angry, he was angry because he himself was looking at going organic (and) he felt that it was going to jeopardise his chances of seeking Soil Association (recognition)".

Other farmers were concerned that they might not get full price for their rape crop as they couldn't guarantee them as GM free because of cross-pollination. Jean sensed a general feeling in the farming community that, as over BSE and salmonella in eggs, they were being led up the garden path once more by the agro-chemical industry. There was anticipation of disaster, despite lack of knowledge of what might lie at the end of the path. Or perhaps because of that ignorance. By coincidence that evening, I picked up a local paper in Swindon with a front-page headline 'Government apologises to GM crop trial farmer'. Indeed, the story was to follow me around for several weeks. The farmer had received an apology for the pressure he was being put under by protesters. The letter admits that no-one knows the impact of GM crops: 'Very simply we want to establish whether or not the use of GM crops is likely to result in positive or negative effects on wildlife, compared to the use of conventional crops.'[88] Jean was quoted as

---

88. *Swindon Evening Advertiser*, 26/5/99

saying it was the local community who should be thanked — "We are taking part in a giant experiment we did not agree to be party to and which we strongly oppose." The 'Comment' column in the paper supported this view: 'Those most deserving of an apology are the people living in this area, who have every right to feel that they haven't been kept adequately informed.' The following Wednesday the *Guardian* published the Friends of the Earth guide to 148 sites throughout the country being used for trials. Not to be outdone, the Archers on BBC Radio 4 was portraying a family split down the middle between supporters and opponents of direct action against GM crop trials.

More startling still was the announcement on BBC1 nine o'clock news on 7 May the same year that Captain Barker of Lushill Farm had been forced to destroy his crop by the trustees of the farm who were holding the property in trust for his children. Presumably they used a weed-killer which the crop had not been genetically modified to resist. A local organic farmer was interviewed and pointed out that pollination by wind meant that there was no way of restricting such a trial to one farm or one field. The local news which followed claimed grandly that the eyes of the world were on a farm near Swindon. While this was probably intended ironically, there is no doubt that the eyes of multinational agro-chemical firms were upon what was going on in Wiltshire, since it is those firms who have most to gain from imposing GM crops on the farming community.

'I'm not a Luddite': on the uses of science and technology

Jean had found out through her computer and the Internet about the food trial at Lushill Farm. She claimed: "I'm not a Luddite, I'm not against mankind using technology to advance certain things, but I am against technological fixes, I am against technology being used when we already have a perfectly good system in place to do things with less environmental impact." As we saw in the previous chapter, Morris too supported the use of technology to banish what he called 'useless toil', but saw no merit in using it for its own sake. A well-made hand-crafted object, fit for its purpose, would last a human lifetime, whereas a cheap, shoddy article from a factory would need replacing within a relatively short time. Eventually, the cheap factory-produced object would cost more in natural resources than the handicraft object. Jean thought it was about time we let our "natural affinity for nature" shine through, a view which she intriguingly described as "the William Morris in me". I added the trite thought: "We know it's wrong but we don't know exactly in what way it's wrong". In retrospect, I consider it both trite and dangerous, and scarcely a thought at all. Many advances in medicine would never have happened if medical researchers had not searched honestly for cures to illnesses which had previously been accepted as part of 'the natural world.' Similarly, contraceptives, which have without any doubt given women more control over their own bodies, are still attacked as being somehow 'against nature'. Jean herself pointed out to me that many genetic scientists who support the use of GMOs in medical work and in laboratory processes do not support their use in food crops. It is up to the scientists to devise tests and trials which do not take unnecessary risks with the environment. While the Government has placed a moratorium on the commercial growing of GM crops, trials continue, and the risk of cross-pollination from those trials is still present. As with nuclear power, knowledge of the technology is not simply going to disappear from the human mind. Forgetting implies a conscious and ongoing effort by society.

On GMOs, little England and William Morris

Of course, risk is not just about environmental issues. Risk also relates very much to the rate of change in a society and the capacity people have to respond to that change. Anthony Giddens has consistently employed the image of change and modernity as a juggernaut. Riding the juggernaut can be exciting and exhilarating, but it creates a world in which people are constantly under stress, constantly assailed by anxieties about what the future holds, and whether they will continue to be able to ride the juggernaut of change. Ulrich Beck has described the way in which education can give us a little more understanding of change, a little more control over our own destinies and those of people close to us. But poorer people who find themselves living next door to a factory, a motorway, or any other source of evil-smelling fumes, have less chance to move away than their wealthier neighbours. They are also likely to have a poorer education than those wealthy neighbours, less likely to possess qualifications that can be traded for secure jobs, and less likely to take part in the necessary retraining and reskilling processes that we call lifelong learning.

In Abingdon itself, education is a class issue. Abingdon and district has at least three private secondary schools in addition to its three state comprehensives. While Radley College is boarders only (£4,550 per term in 1998) and serves a national market, the School of St Helen and St Katherine (girls) is just a day-school, while Abingdon School (boys) is over eighty percent day boys. Fees were, respectively, £1,654 and £1,982 per term. The contrast may not be quite as dramatic as between Eton and the Slough comprehensives, but the same possibility exists of buying your way out of at least some of the uncertainties of the modern world. In the same way, our control over the food we eat is much increased if we can afford to stock up at Sainsbury's every few weeks, or even patronise the local organic food shop. And people in Abingdon who are suspicious of mainstream medicine can buy into the services of two osteopaths, two acupuncturists, one homeopath, two reflexologists, two aromatherapists and one chiropractor.

Our capacity to deal with the risks we cannot see would be greatly enhanced if we all understood a little more about science. Enough, that is, to see when the wool is being pulled too blatantly across our eyes. Sometimes, as with GM crops, it is a matter of understanding scientific method, and the importance of exhaustive testing before new products and processes are made generally available. Sometimes, as with radioactive waste, we need access to experts whose private monitoring can complement the 'official' figures churned out, not to inform us, but to reassure us blandly that 'all is well'. In Abingdon, support for this view comes from an unexpected direction. Just outside Abingdon lies the village of Marcham, and in Marcham is Denman College, since 1948 the residential college of the National Federation of Women's Institutes (NFWI). Yet this should not be unexpected, given that the WI began in Canada as the result of a baby dying from drinking infected milk. The education and training of rural women and their preparation for public life was its purpose from the outset.

Since 1990 the NFWI has been involved in a substantial project to increase public understanding of science. In one of those ironies so typical of political democracies, the same government which is reluctant to give us full information about air pollution, radioactivity or GMOs, has set up a Committee on the Public Understanding of Science (COPUS) which supports activities like that of the NFWI. The basic process is the cascade conference — national events from which members take information and ideas back to their local groups. As Margaret Nicholson, the National Education Officer of NFWI, says, it is about "finding ways into science through everyday life — the water we drink, the food we eat, the chemicals we use to wash our clothes, the medicines we take". The WI voice is there alongside more explicitly environmental organisations such as Friends of the Earth helping us to fight back against all those who are trying to mortgage out future for the sake of profit.

Morris was very conscious of England as a small country, a carefully nurtured countryside which could only be meddled with at great potential cost to its inhabitants. He noted that nature as we experience it in everyday life was more often than not the result of the interaction between human kind and a more primitive state of nature. At the same time, he was one of the first thinkers to put forward a serious argument for leaving at least some areas free from human interference, in a state of wilderness. There is little evidence that Morris knew much science. At the same time, he was an avid experimenter, especially in the use of natural substances in dyeing. His letters bear witness to an amazing ability to explore patiently the properties of the living world and the ways these might be used by people within craft processes and in ways which would not impact adversely on the fragile environment.

An increasing number of writers have turned back to Morris as part of the search for a more sustainable way of conducting human affairs. Adam Buick has argued that the 'communist' economy of *News from Nowhere* — using communist in the non-pejorative sense of a co-operative, non-profit system balancing inputs and outputs in harmony with nature — is an 'ecological imperative':

> Humans are a part of nature, but a part that has yet to find a stable niche in the ecology of the biosphere... Sooner or later, humanity must establish a stable, sustainable relationship with the rest of nature, one where its needs on a world scale, and what it takes from the rest of nature to satisfy them, would be in balance with the capacity of the biosphere to renew itself after supplying them.[89]

We need to look again at Morris, thinking of the deep message which lies behind the cheerful, natural patterns of his

89. Adam Buick, 'A market by the way: the economics of nowhere', in (eds) S. Coleman and P. O'Sullivan, *William Morris and News from Nowhere: a vision for our time* (Green Books, 1990), pp.151-168

designs, and the light tread of the inhabitants of *Nowhere* upon the surface of the earth.

Chapter 8
Oxford — two cities for the price of one

The illusions in question boil down to the belief that the 'messiness' of the human world is but a temporary state and repairable state, sooner or later to be replaced by the orderly and systematic rule of reason. The truth in question is that the messiness will stay whatever we do or know, that the little orders and systems we carve out in the world are brittle, until-further-notice, and as arbitrary and in the end as contingent as their alternatives. (Zygmunt Bauman)[90]

When I remember the contrast between the Oxford of today and the Oxford which I first saw thirty years ago, I wonder I can face the misery... of visiting it. (William Morris, 1883)

Introduction

Inequalities of wealth and poverty, culture, work and risk have dominated the central chapters of the book. In these last three chapters, as we reach the upper reaches of the river, there is a shift of emphasis towards those forms of association, community and solidarity which have the potential to produce a more optimistic future. If an over-emphasis on individualism places at risk our very existence as a species, what forms of community might yet save us? And by save us I mean allow the expression of personal identity within a framework of rights and responsibilities, rather than a framework of egalitarian oppression, which has been the outcome of so many revolutionary projects in the twentieth century.

In some ways, I have always known Oxford, although I

---

90. Zygmunt Bauman, *Postmodern ethics*, (Blackwell, 1993) pp.32-33

was a grown man with a baby in tow when I visited it for the first time during one of those hot, parched summers of the mid 1970s. At grammar school, getting a place at 'Oxbridge' was regarded as the highest objective. While there was a strong element of social snobbery and elitism in that, there was also some notion of an expansive, educational regime in which scholarship was seen as an end in itself rather than the more routine, utilitarian education on offer at newer universities. Oxford invites, but Oxford also rejects, as Hardy's Jude and Willy Russell's Rita found to their cost. It is not just the beauty of its mellow cloisters, its graceful towers, spires and pinnacles, the delicate light on Cotswold stone (how hard it is to write about Oxford without using clichés) — it is also that dreadful sense of exclusion and inferiority that it inspires in people. My guide-book is typical. Titled the *Clarendon Guide to Oxford*, it manages not to mention anything in Oxford which is not part of the university.[91] We shall construct a rather different map of Oxford.

Morris and Oxford One

Morris and Oxford go together, as older car-drivers will remember. Indeed, I think I failed completely to explain to at least one person in Oxford that my subject of 'William Morris and social change' related to the nineteenth century writer, designer and socialist William Morris rather than to Sir William Richard Morris. Affectionately known as Billy, he later became Lord Nuffield and was the benefactor of Oxford's Nuffield College. The man who began life with a small bicycle shop ended life as a mass manufacturer of motor-cars and a very rich man. Indeed, the fellows of Nuffield College, dedicated to exchange between academic research and the world of

---

91. A.R. Woolley, *The Clarendon guide to Oxford*, second edition (Oxford University Press, 1972)

'practical affairs', give a rather good notion of what still constitutes the 'establishment' in this country. My 1972 edition of the Clarendon guide notes that they have included:

> chairmen of great industrial concerns, former members of the Cabinet and Civil Service, Trade Union leaders, a speaker of the House of Commons, an Adviser to the Bank of England, and the Chairman of the Atomic Energy Authority

But 'our' William Morris's relationship with Oxford is as complex and fascinating as the no doubt equally fascinating story of the King of Cowley.

Morris, as Fiona MacCarthy explains in some detail in her biography, was intended to be a priest in the Church of England. As a student, he moved from his evangelical background towards the high church of the so-called 'Oxford Movement' with its strong emphasis on ritual and liturgy, and its confirmation of Gothic as the true style of church architecture. The 'Oxford Movement' was, of course, to become a lucrative source of income for Morris and Co. in later years. Its emphasis on ritual demanded stained glass, vestments, altar cloths, chalices and crosses. Something of the flavour of the Anglo-Catholic world of Morris's Oxford circle, which already included Burne-Jones, is to be found on a CD called 'Music for William Morris', created for the 1996 centenary exhibition at the Victoria and Albert Museum.[92] It includes six hymns from the Sarum Rite, in use in churches in England from the thirteenth century until the 1550s. We know that Morris was a member of the Plainsong Society while a student at Exeter College in the early 1850s. When Morris began work in the offices of the architect G.E. Street, he would certainly have known John Sedding, brother of Edmund Sedding whose 'Antient Christmas Carols' was published

---

92. 'Music for William Morris', Isis Records, CD020

in 1860. Morris produced the English words for carol number eight, 'Masters in this hall':

> Nowell! Nowell! Nowell!
> Nowell sing we loud
> God today hath poor folk rais'd
> And cast adown the proud

As Christine Poulson has recently pointed out,[93] the line of development is not just a simple matter of turning from high church Anglicanism to a medievalism shorn of its religious content. For a start, she reminds us that Morris, following Ruskin, continued throughout his life to be concerned with key values of 'duty, conscience and hard work' reflecting the low church background he had been brought up in. Further, that from about 1855 both Morris and Burne-Jones were attracted to that special English brand of Christian socialism which combined high church ritual with a concern for the poor and oppressed, and how brotherhood and community might find form in the sprawling industrial towns and cities. Poulson quotes from a much later letter in which Morris writes that at Oxford he had been

> a good deal influenced by the works of Charles Kingsley, and got into my head therefrom some socio-political ideas which would have developed probably but for the attractions of art and poetry.

But the attractions were not just art and poetry but girls too — girls as models, girls as fun, girls as sex partners. Oxford was not just where Morris and his friends began to formulate views about art, design and society which were to have a major impact on the second half of the nineteenth century, but also the location in which Morris and his friends formulated a cosy, medievalist, male

---

93. Christine Poulson, 'Burne-Jones, Morris and God', *Journal of the William Morris Society*, volume 13, No.1, 1998, pp.45-54

view of fraternity which he later tried to apply more widely to society. But did it ever really apply to his women? If *News from Nowhere* and the later romances gives a more positive role to women than was normal in Victorian society, it is scarcely convincing to a modern reader. In general, the women serve while the men get on with 'the business', whether rowing, talking, working in the fields or putting the world to rights. It is scarcely a utopian prospect for fifty-one percent of the human race.[94] Morris continually emphasises the sexual allure of his female characters in a way which reflects what Julia Swindells and Lisa Jardine have called the 'saccharin delusions of the male mind'.[95] Swindells and Jardine go on to show how Morris's marriage to Jane Burden, plucked from the Oxford working-class by the Morris group, has been treated as some sort of artistic enterprise rather than as a statement about gender and class relations in Victorian England. This is how MacCarthy describes Jane's background:

> Janey belonged to the substratum of Oxford society recreated some years later in Thomas Hardy's *Jude the Obscure*. She was born in 1839 in St Helen's Passage off Holywell, in a cramped and insanitary cottage; her mother registered her birth not with a signature but with a cross, indicating illiteracy. Janey's father was a stablehand or ostler at Symonds' Livery Stables in Holywell Street. Her older brother William was working as a college messenger by the age of 14. Her older sister Mary Anne died of tuberculosis in 1849.[96]

94. Ernest Belfort Bax, co-editor with Morris of *Commonweal*, co-author with him of *Socialism: its growth and outcome* (1893) and Morris's tutor in Marxist economics, seriously argued against votes for women on the grounds that it would create a dictatorship based on their numerical superiority in society. See E.P. Thompson, *William Morris: romantic to revolutionary*, p.374
95. Julia Swindells and Lisa Jardine, *What's left? Women in culture and the labour movement*, chapter 3, 'Writing history with a vengeance: getting good Marx with William Morris (and Jane's Burden)', p.58
96. MacCarthy, p. 136

While it is by no means my claim that conditions in Oxford at the end of the twentieth century were identical to those in the slums of mid-nineteenth century Oxford, there are nevertheless forces at work which are producing similar kinds of inequality and social exclusion. A widely publicised research study published in 1994 was reported in the press as demonstrating that Oxford was now poorer than Oldham.[97] In particular, that one in four children in Oxford lived in households dependent on income support. More generally, the report underlined the growing contrasts between rich and poor in Oxford as in other towns.

Morris and Oxford Two

Lying to the south side of the High Street, University College Oxford lays claim to being the oldest foundation in the University. More obscurely, it traces its origins back to King Alfred. No doubt modern scholars have as much fun proving or disproving this theory as their medieval predecessors had in arguing about whether the world was flat, round, or definitively pear-shaped. In 1999, while other universities were bidding for government money to employ staff to 'widen participation' to groups and classes under-represented in higher education, University College was employing someone to raise another few million pounds from its alumni to develop the college in unspecified ways. 'Robinson' passed this way on his second journey, although he showed little interest in Oxford as a seat of learning. He was apparently more interested in the Cowley Works, of which more later, and the Campsfield Detention Centre, where asylum seekers are held in prison conditions pending their appeals. He did pause to mention that Oxford was the King's capital in the Civil War and

---

97. Michael Noble et al, *Changing patterns of income and wealth in Oxford and Oldham* (University of Oxford Department of Applied Social Studies and Social Research, 1994)

'Hitler's preferred capital had he occupied England'. He compared the 'disorientation and disillusionment' of the modern period to Robert Burton's *Anatomy of Melancholy* of 1621. Burton was librarian of Christ Church and Vicar of St Thomas the Martyr 1616-39. I fancy that neither Robinson nor his creator cared much for Oxford University.

In July 1883 Morris (our Morris) returned to Oxford to receive a fellowship at Exeter College, where he had been an undergraduate. Later in the year he was invited to make a speech at University College which not only effectively ended his relationship with the University but also marked his public 'coming out' as a socialist. His title was 'Art and democracy', though it was later published as *Art under plutocracy*. By all accounts, the University authorities found it barely comprehensible that one of their number had gone over to what was seen as the dangerous and subversive foreign doctrine of socialism. Ruskin was in the chair. His view was that amelioration of the living conditions of the poor could be obtained through a process of enlightenment directed by the ruling class. No doubt that view was able to encompass Morris's opening remarks on the damage done to the fabric of Oxford by industrialisation:

> When I remember the contrast between the Oxford of today and the Oxford which I first saw thirty years ago, I wonder I can face the misery... of visiting it, even to have the honour of addressing you tonight. But furthermore, not only are the cities a disgrace to us, and the smaller towns a laughing-stock; not only are the dwellings of man grown inexpressibly base and ugly, but the very cowsheds and cart-stables, nay, the merest piece of necessary farm-engineering, are tarred with the same brush.

But like a fundamentalist preacher, Morris was up and running. He then turns to the impact of human kind on the environment, the requirement of careful husbandry of farmland and a plea for the conservation of wilderness, a purple passage which is quoted at some length in the next chapter of this book. He confesses his own conversion to the cause of socialism, and attacks the competitive capitalist system in terms of waste, anarchy and warfare. He then turns to hope and courage, recurring themes in later Morris — hope that people will come to understand what is being done to them and courage to unite in order to design and realise an alternative future:

> It may be that in England the mass of the working classes has no hope; that it will not be hard to keep them down for a while, possibly a long while. The hope that this may be so I will say plainly is a dastard's hope, for it is founded on the chance of their degradation. I say such an expectation is that of slave-holders or the hangers-on of slave-holders. I believe, however, that hope is growing among the working classes even in England; at any rate you may be sure of one thing, that there is at least discontent. Can any of us doubt that, since there is unjust suffering? Or which of us would be contented with ten shillings a week to keep our households with, or to dwell in unutterable filth and have to pay the price of good lodging for it? Do you doubt that if we had any time for it amidst our struggle to live we should look into the title of those who kept us there, themselves rich and comfortable, under the pretext that it was necessary to society? I tell you there is plenty of discontent, and I call on all those who think there is something better than making money for the sake of making it to help in <u>educating that discontent into hope</u>, that is into the demand for the new birth of society; and I do this not because I am afraid of it, but because I myself am discontented and long for justice (my emphasis)

We are coming close now to the thought of another major thinker who passed this way; Raymond Williams. His thought is as central to the twentieth century as Morris's was to the nineteenth century, and almost as widely focussed. Rather than trace Williams' own links with Morris and the tradition of nineteenth century critical social thinking, a path that other writers have already passed down, I want to pursue the connection with Morris and hope in relation to Williams' last book, *Towards 2000*.[98] It seems particularly appropriate to do so, in a book being published in the year 2000.

Williams begins his essay 'Resources for a journey of hope' by pointing out that it is not just idealistic leftists who are plotting the future. He refers to a group of determined and hard-nosed international businessmen and politicians who are planning a future based on the concept of 'strategic' advantage. All thought of human and social purpose is subordinated to the need to keep one step ahead of other countries, other businesses, 'our competitors' in the broadest sense. Williams describes this future as Plan X. Against it he places the existence of what he calls 'resources of hope', based on developing scientific knowledge around ecology and the environment, and the existence of campaigning groups committed to a saner, more human future. We noted the existence of a number of such people in the previous chapter, in relation to the debates around nuclear and genetically modified food risks. We hear Morris talking in Williams' enthusiasm for 'the new emphases on durability, reclamation, maintenance and economy of resources'. He proposes taking advantage of labour-saving devices in some aspects of our lives, in order to shift resources towards labour-intensive activities such as the care of the elderly and the sick. He concludes:

> It is only in a shared belief and insistence that there are practical alternatives that the balance of forces and chances begins to alter. Once the inevitabilities are challenged, we begin gathering our resources for a journey of hope. If there are no easy answers there are still available and discoverable hard answers, and it is these that we can now learn to make and share.

We are still learning.

---

98. Raymond Williams, *Towards 2000* (Hogarth Press, 1983)

A year after the publication of *Towards 2000,* Williams returned to the attack with an interview included in the very fine and provocative catalogue of the 1984 Morris exhibition 'William Morris Today' at the Institute of Contemporary Arts.[99] On the one hand, he refers back to Morris's principles of 'meaning in work' ("Yet the thing that comes through most to the late twentieth century… was this emphasis on meaning in work"). On the other hand, he criticises Morris for his lack of attention to other forms of work and creativity in a way that draws on feminist criticisms of the masculine bias in much thinking on the left:

> "But there is then also the huger area of work, which is not now called work as most of it is not paid employment, in which people are looking after other people. In that area we can find a lot of the best meanings. Yet both Morris and Ruskin, for personal reasons, were relatively blind to this; to women, for example, where the notion of creativity has an additional dimension because this has been creativity with people rather than just with materials."

'Educating discontent into hope' must include a demythologising of the past and a vivid and imaginative understanding of the present and the many little steps which may eventually build into a broad highway to the future, but which in the meantime can offer meaning and purpose to our fragmented lives.

Oxford — car city

Much earlier in his life, Raymond Williams also wrote a novel about Oxford. Less autobiographical than his earlier *Border Country*, which was set in and around the village of Pandy on the Wales/England border where Williams grew

99. *William Morris today* (ICA, 1984)

up, *Second Generation*[100] nevertheless reflects some of Williams' own concern about his uprooting from a settled working-class community into a fluid, de-centred academic environment. Peter Owen is the son of working class parents who have moved to Oxford from Wales. His father is a shop steward in the Cowley car factory, his mother a Labour Party activist. Peter himself is a post-graduate student at the University. The author's description of the sanitised, rational space of the car factory is memorable not just in its own terms, but because as Williams himself came to recognise, it is precisely that world of organised certainty that has disappeared and that has given rise to a much more dangerous world in which people struggle to identify purpose and meaning, as we shall see below:

> It is large enough to impose its own rhythms: a place of lines and regular intervals, an area rubbed clean and newly designed. It is not the huddle of mills to the course of a river, or the squat of colliery workings to the line of a seam. It needs no natural features; it is simply a working space that has been cleared and set in order, giving room to move.[101]

In order to get some feel for the past of the car industry in Oxford, I talked to Ivor Brough, who had been a shop steward at Cowley. The first surprise was that Ivor, apprenticed at a tailor's in the High Street aged fourteen and recruited by Morris Motors six years later (in 1950) had never worked on a production line. He worked exclusively on the seats, ending up as the man who went round the work putting up safety padding so that other workers would not bang their heads on iron girders and the like. At first, working in the trim shop brought him into close contact with older, working-class women who 'teased me unmercifully': 'you imagine me, a young man, very slim,

---

100. Raymond Williams, *Second generation* (Hogarth Press, 1964)
101. *Second generation*, 1988 edition, p.10, quoted in Tony Pinkney, *Raymond Williams* (Seren Books, 1991) p.53

blond, right in the middle of a line of women'. His mates called him Snowy because of his platinum blond hair. In the years after the Second World War, the Morris works at Cowley had a head start over much of the European car industry, which was still recovering from the war. They paid well, in comparison for example with unskilled labouring or domestic work around the University, and the unions had an easy time of it. Ivor confirmed Williams' point in *Second generation* that the unions were mainly concerned with local issues. The perspectives of other factories, let alone of the overall business position of the firm, and the failure to balance workers' demands and shareholders' demands with the need to invest satisfactorily in new designs and products, only come into view in retrospect.

In view of what is coming later in this chapter about the disastrous impact of the run-down of the Cowley plant on the life of at least one working-class community in Oxford (Blackbird Leys), the most interesting parts of Ivor Brough's story are those concerning the years after he was made redundant in 1976. With plenty of notice, he was able to plan for the future by turning a work-related hobby, upholstery, into a satisfactory business. He operated first from his garage, then a workshop 'out in the country', then a new garage in an extension to his house, and now in a small Swiss chalet-style garden shed. For much of the time he worked two days a week for Oriel College on upholstery and odd jobs. One job the whole family remembers concerned the curtains that covered two sides of the dining-room at Nuffield College, a special request of the Bursar, who thought that yellow stimulated good conversation and lively argument. His daughter Alison Noel still remembers 'mum making acres and acres of lemon velvet curtains' — Molly Brough's part of the family business was always the curtains. I introduced the idea of retirement, but without success: 'I understand what you're saying, but to me, I've got my hobby back, upholstery was my hobby.'

The unacceptable face of global Thatcherism

In 1991, the Blackbird Leys estate, next door to the Cowley car-works, erupted in riots. The estate had been developed in the 1940s predominantly to satisfy housing need at the car factory, people much like Peter Owen's family in *Second Generation*. Beatrix Campbell described Blackbird Leys in *Goliath: Britain's dangerous places*, published two years after the riots in Cardiff, Oxford and on Tyneside, as a model estate of predominantly small semi-detached houses and gardens, with good relations between black and white people, unlike the other estates she looked at. At the same time,

> Blackbird Leys was a terminus, the end of the road eastwards out of Oxford, past the Rover motor car factory at Cowley. Cowley and Blackbird Leys are the alter ego of Oxford, a city synonymous with intellectual industry and tradition. It was a topography corrugated by brick factories, steel chimneys and pleasant suburban estates.[102]

Her account of the estate both feeds from and feeds into the moral panic which coalesced in England in the 90s into the notion of the 'underclass'. She saw this as a new sort of people, largely excluded from the labour market, dependent on state benefits, prone to drug-taking and petty crime, often formed into non-traditional family structures (especially the family headed up by a single woman), and, crucially, reproducing itself from one generation to the next. This we know now to be substantially untrue. People move in and out of unemployment, benefit dependency, drug dependency and crime. Nevertheless, this myth of the underclass has been frequently cited as an 'explanation' of the havoc wreaked on society by Margaret Thatcher and the restructuring of British capitalism. It also obscures the aspect of the problem which Campbell

---

102. Beatrix Campbell, *Goliath: Britain's dangerous places* (Methuen, 1993) pp.31-32

brings out most vividly: this was a male problem. In the early 1970s, for example, thirty thousand people were employed in manufacturing in Oxford, ninety percent of them male; by 1990 that figure had declined to five thousand, a mere five percent of the Oxford workforce.

The key to understanding the 1991 events in Blackbird Leys was a group of young men who stole cars and used them for nightly displays of driving skills in the central part of the estate. This is how Campbell describes them:

> The night boys defied the definition of a passive under-class; these young men weren't <u>under</u> anyone. Economically they were spare, surplus; personally they were dependant on someone else for their upkeep, usually their mother; socially they were fugitives, whose lawlessness kept them inside and yet outside their own community. They had no jobs, no incomes, no property, no cars, no responsibilities.[103]

At its height, nightime joy-riding became a popular spectator sport, growing from 'attendances' of thirty to forty in 1990 to a peak of one hundred in 1991. People brought deckchairs and refreshments to enjoy the spectacle. The activity even had its own intellectuals, in the form of the authors of a Situationist manifesto circulating on the estate which claimed:

> In taking performance cars and making them perform, the joyriders demonstrate the only proper use of all technology — its use for fun. To live as we choose we must suppress those who choose how we live.[104]

Everybody knew what was going on, but nobody took action. The general view was that this was a crisis of 'order' rather than 'law'. People on the estate, according to Campbell, acknowledged the noise and nuisance being created by the lads, but viewed the crime of stealing cars as a minor offence,

---

103. Campbell, p.29
104. In Campbell, p.45

because of compulsory car insurance. When the police acted, they came down on the people of Blackbird Leys very heavily indeed, occupying the area for a week, during which eighty-three people were arrested, mostly for breach of the peace or other minor public order offences. While there are elements in this story which are new, there are also references back to Victorian moral panics which would have been all too familiar to Morris: moral panics about the 'mob', the undeserving poor excluded from regular employment and living in a twilight world between legality and crime.

Making progress out of chaos?

Blackbird Leys on a sunny day at the turn of the century does not feel like either a modern or a Victorian slum. It is true that the central area of the estate is uninspiring. Marked by the only two tower blocks, there are a number of dull public buildings such as the Blackbird Leys site of Oxford College, a Catholic church, and the Housing Centre, which also acts as the base of the Claimants' Union. The shops have the usual hangers-on in the form of a small group of alcoholics, young people arguing loudly, a few pale children being shouted at by harassed mothers. And of course, speed humps everywhere — the most obvious legacy of those days of anarchy in the summer of 1991. Yet far from being abandoned, Blackbird Leys has grown substantially during the 1990s, and acquired a largish new area of mixed housing, some of it private, some of it rented — in the new jargon 'social housing' rather than 'council housing' — put up by Housing Associations keen to encourage participation and happy, smiling tenants.

A further feature of the newer part of Blackbird Leys is the generous provision of social facilities. The most striking of these is The Barn. This is a copy of the original old converted stone farm barn on the site, which was found to be too old and rotten to be done up. It is a general-purpose community building used for activities as diverse as aerobics, karate, parties and meetings. The Dovecote, again with obvious references back to pre-industrial times in its rather free adaptation of vernacular design, is managed by a worker from the Blackbird Leys Community Development Initiative, and is an under 8s and families centre. The remaining two public buildings are The Farmhouse which is used as a base for the Housing Association's support team for vulnerable people and The Clockhouse, which is used for activities for older residents. There is a brand new school on this newer part of the estate, in a more authentically twentieth century functional style. It is an idyllic scene in the hot June sunshine at going home time — white, black and Asian children and mums trailing homewards, a sight that might be seen anywhere in the country from leafy suburb to inner city estate to country village. Very different from the stressful morning scenes in the shopping centre on the older part of the estate.

It would be wrong, though, to draw a picture of some kind of urban idyll; of the English finally coming to terms with life in the city, albeit with a rural heritage veneer. Anti-climb paint to discourage kids from climbing onto the slate roofs is much in evidence. The Clockhouse bears a smart sign announcing that it was opened in 1997 by Hilary Armstrong, the local government minister. It also bears another: 'Concealed CCTV cameras operate on these premises. These premises are alarmed.' This in turn contrasts with the friendly notices on the door advertising the Credit Union, a disputes surgery run by Community Mediation, a pre-school car-boot sale. The signs indicate the sources of external support — the European Social Fund, the Church Urban Fund and BBC Children in Need. There is also evidence, both in Blackbird Leys and nearby, of activity designed to teach people new skills and equip them for some of the newer jobs now beginning to emerge in Oxford. There is not just the College, but also the Pathways Training Centre, while just off the estate is the Cowley Training Centre. The Centre is in a little road called Bobby Fryer Close. The staff at the Centre kindly provided me with a copy of an *Oxford Times* article on Bobby Fryer, emphasising his lesser known status as a Jewish exile from Hitler's Austria rather than the man who for twenty years was the senior shop steward of the Transport and General Workers' Union at Cowley.

As so often on this journey up the Thames, the old and the new sit comfortably together in post-modern confusion. Blackbird Leys butts onto the remaining car factory on the old Pressed Steel site east of the ring road, while the Business Park developments are going up on land released by the car industry east of the ring road. The car factory has revived the old name of Rover which has no Oxford connections at all, while the new industrial buildings of the Business Park are in that design idiom already so familiar from Slough and Reading and Abingdon with their pitched roofs and handsome red bricks. Even the new speaks the language of the old. Alison Noel remembers seeing "blokes walking up and down with hands behind their backs watching the demolition going on", watching their identities being torn away from them, or some, like her father, happily entering into a new one.

According to local mythology, one demolished area adjacent to the ring road was intended to be a big showroom for BMW who now own Rover. It is an ambiguous relationship. In 1998 BMW threatened to take the Longbridge work from Birmingham to Hungary unless the Government forked out more subsidy. Afterwards, the Hungarians said that such a move had never been on the cards. Now BMW has sold Longbridge for £1. Alison and I wondered about all that money spent subsidising unnecessary motor-car production that we don't really need — back to Morris again. What other jobs might have been created using that degree of state support? I also reflected on the large brownfield sites still waiting to be redeveloped here in Oxford city, while Abingdon and other Oxfordshire towns and villages continue to develop their brand new science parks and industrial estates on greenfield sites. But there are smart new premises for Blackwell's Publishers at the entrance to the estate, while down the road, cheek-by-jowl with the car factory, are high tech industries, diverted north to Oxford from the M4 corridor by its academic prestige and well-qualified professional labour force.

As in most English towns and cities, sport, too, is public policy as well as popular entertainment and big business. On the one hand there is the Blackbird Leys Leisure Centre, so good that it attracts people from all over Oxford. Outside it looks rather forbidding, with minimum windows for security reasons, but inside on a weekday afternoon a busy representation of the new multi-ethnic England. There are numerous special concessions for claimants, students and older people, emphasising the social purposes of the centre. And this brings us to Oxford United Football Club. As a football-mad boy in Somerset, I depended on live rather than televised football for my entertainment. One of the best matches I saw each season was between Bath City and what was then called Headington United (after the Oxford suburb) who in those days often fought out the Southern League title between them. While Bath City languish at Twerton Park, from which particular condescension of history the film director Ken Loach is attempting to rescue them, Oxford United have become a Football League club whose affairs became deeply embroiled with the complex business activities of publisher and one-time Labour MP, Robert Maxwell.

Within sight of Blackbird Leys lies a half-built stadium which may or may not eventually become the home of Oxford United Football Club. While the Madejski Stadium in Reading represents the successful side of the new world of football-as-consumption, the events surrounding the new and as yet unnamed stadium in Oxford represent many of the unacceptable choices which globalised capital tries to force on the world. The whole package to complete the stadium hinged on obtaining planning for a multiplex cinema and hotel to be built on the site. Readers will remember that the hotel and conference centre were integral parts of the Madejski 'package' in Reading. Complex negotiations were going on between the London-based hotel firm which owns the Football Club and the City Council. The problem was a perplexing one: on the one hand the prospects of jobs, entertainment and liveliness; on the other a further increase in traffic movements within and around a city which is already in danger of choking on its traffic fumes, and little advantage to those people who still get around by public transport, on foot and by bicycle.

As I drive off the estate, I am tempted to look in a journalistic way for burnt-out cars. Yes, I did see one. But Blackbird Leys did look lovely in the sun. On a stretch of parched grass there is the conventional 'No ball games allowed' sign — with a happy game of soccer going on beneath it.

Blackbird Leys itself, as already suggested, is like a giant social test-bed for ideas about community development, and how the social and the community and the local can somehow be integrated back into the global picture which has dominated my journey on these central stretches of the Thames. Community development has many strands, and there are many ties and links between them. Firstly, there are those strands that deal with children. A major thread of the Blackbird Leys Community Development Initiative is provision for under 8s and their parents. In turn this relates to the low levels of achievement of children at school. An education action zone is being set up to try and bring this up to something more like the national average. But learning is not just for the youngsters. There is also concern to offer education and training to people who by and large expected little of the formal education system, who got little out of it, and are now firmly at the bottom of the social heap, in insecure part-time and informal work if not unemployed, and almost always dependent on some form of state benefit. Then there are the 'culture of poverty' groups — people such as the Credit Union, the Claimants' Union and the

LETS (local exchange trading scheme) which seek to help local people make the best of their frugal resources. A further strand of Community Development is work with older people, who often feel bruised and angry about the changes and upheavals of recent years. Finally, and potentially tying it all together, is the work of the group who produce *Leys News*, a lively and free community newspaper which gets into most of the households on the estate.

Communications is an issue on the estate, where so many households simply survive in an isolated way. Sue Cooper of the Ealing Family Housing Association has produced a report on the estate in which she comprehensively outlines both the problems and the prospects for change. Despite a broadly based Steering Group, a questionnaire sent to every home with *Leys News* generated only sixty replies out of five thousand delivered. Only one percent of people on the estate were sufficiently convinced that the exercise was 'for real' to feel that it was worthwhile replying. So most of the material came from discussions by focus groups of community activists plus people doing paid and voluntary work on the estate. Many residents remain disengaged and have very low expectations of what can be done, despite the investment in the estate.

Sue presented her report at an event called 'the Community Lunch', a chance for people living and working in and around the estate to meet and chat. These are held regularly, usually sitting around in a hall eating sandwiches with people leading discussions about different issues connected with Blackbird Leys. They bring together community activists with a wide range of professionals such as health visitors, social workers, community workers, school and college teachers, childcare and youth workers. There were maybe too many white, middle-class professionals, too few people who lived on the estate, although a minority were there as secretaries or chairs of local organisations. Despite the fact that one of the main themes of the report is how to draw together the various threads of work on the estate, there seemed a curious reluctance to engage with the priorities suggested. The problems still seem big, the resources to solve them small. Another concern, which Sue expressed herself, was that community development involved 'asking vulnerable people to run their own services' — how could they support, and indeed, pay people for the work they do? To me, this seemed a central question, and it was encouraging to see the LETS scheme being viewed in this light. People would earn credits for voluntary community work which they could then use to buy in other goods and services for their households.

Community work must have some vision of the future as well as the present, if it is to be effective, and link the 'personal troubles' people experience in their everyday lives with the 'public issues' debated so noisily in politics and the media. As Jim Crowther and Mae Shaw have put it: 'Community work should be concerned with the world as it should be as much as the world as it is'[105] It is another way of describing Oscar Wilde's criticism of 'a map of the world that does not contain Utopia', quoted at the head of chapter six. Even when you have added into the community development equation on Blackbird Leys the question of jobs and economic development, there still remain persistent and troubling questions about purpose and meaning in work — the very sorts of questions that William Morris and Raymond Williams ask so persistently.

There is too the question of how cultural difference can be added into the equation. Ten percent of the people on Blackbird Leys are from ethnic minorities. Oxford is home to the Campsfield Detention Centre, which itself has seen rioting during the 1990s. Oxfam started here and is now a major employer in the city — its tentacles spread out to embrace not just projects in the countries of the South but also those in the North damaged by precisely the same

---

105. Jim Crowther and Mae Shaw, 'Social movements and the education of desire', *Community Development Journal*, volume 32, No. 3, 1997

global economic forces which see private wealth as always 'good' and public investment as always 'bad'. So arguments about community are complex arguments which refer not to a homogenous geographical bunch of people but to different ethnic and cultural groups. Within Blackbird Leys, people will identify at different times with different communities, the community of the school their children attend, an ethnic group, a church or mosque, the people who live in a single street or block of flats, members of a an interest group or action group which may include people from a wide area. In global terms, the North can learn from the South too. In Oxford, the Development Education Centre are using techniques developed by radical educators in the South to develop community work with black communities in the city, building on the experience of black people in the city including the endemic racism they encounter in their daily lives. It is worth remembering that for some years after the war, the Cowley car-works operated a colour-bar, despite the fact that many of the early migrants were West Indians de-mobbed from RAF bases in the area — men who had risked their lives in the war against fascism.

Morris, inequality and fellowship

It is all very well for E.P. Thompson to find in Morris's socialism 'a moral logic as well as an economic logic' in which there is a stark contrast between 'the ethics of competition, the energies of war' and 'the ethics of co-operation, the energies of love.'[106] Of all the concepts inherited from the eighteenth century Enlightenment, 'fraternity' is the one most in need of re-thinking. It is not clear to me that we even have a term that can be used without embarrassment. Social inclusion — but on whose terms? Soli-

---

106. E.P. Thompson, 'The Communism of William Morris', *ICA catalogue*, 1984, pp.133-34

darity — but is this only against some other persons or group? Fraternity — but what about the women? Fellowship — but isn't this too exclusive? Community — but isn't this too loose? And through all this sticky mess runs the apprehension that the 'cake' we attempt to share out is in itself rotten, an apprehension that leads back to Morris again:

> Like all socialists, Morris was deeply concerned with poverty, squalor, low wages and bad conditions. But he never saw the simple amelioration of bad conditions and poverty as being the first or major aim of socialism. Socialism was about the changes in possibilities, opportunities and forms of life that would follow from a change of control — a change that would not only move control of the means of production from the few to the people, but would also shift control of the purposes of production. He never saw socialism as being simply to do with a re-distribution of existing wealth, or more of the same, but for everybody.[107]

As ever, Morris helps to sort out the problem, but leaves the solution to us: 'To do nothing but grumble and not to act, that is throwing away one's life.'

---

107. Nicholas Pearson, 'The unacceptable Morris', *ICA catalogue*, 1984, p.88

Chapter 9
Kelmscott and the English Countryside

June
See, we have left our hopes and fears behind
To give our very hearts up unto thee;
What better place than this then could we find
By this sweet stream that knows not of the sea,
That guesses not the city's misery,
This little stream whose hamlets scarce have names,
This far-off, lonely mother of the Thames.
(William Morris, *The Earthly Paradise*)

The blackbirds sing at Kelmscott after they have fallen
silent elsewhere. (J. M. Mackail)[108]

Much that has been won after a long struggle has been
trodden upon: we seem no more advanced than when
William Morris was striving to enlighten the masses
nearly a century ago! (Robin Tanner)[109]

Introduction

Kelmscott Manor is without doubt a destination. The
woodcut which forms the frontispiece of the Kelmscott
Press (1892) edition of *News from Nowhere* states clearly
that 'This is the picture of the old house by the Thames to
which the people of the story went. Hereafter follows the
book itself which is called *News from Nowhere* or an Epoch
of Rest.' It is a possible destination, but not the only possible one.

Morris might have chosen the great tithe barn across
the fields at Great Coxwell, a building that is so important

108. J.M. Mackail, *The life of William Morris*, volume 1, chapter 7
109. Robin Tanner, *Double harness, an autobiography by Robin Tanner,
teacher and etcher* (Impact Books, 1987), p.211

to his architectural theories: a great space formed by craftsmen rather than engineers. Yet perhaps he was aware of the socially conservative aspect of such buildings. Tithes involved the demands of the established Church to a tenth part of the produce of the land, a system derided by Chaucer and still a bone of contention in nineteenth century England. There is a compartmentalisation in Morris's thought — the aesthetic positives of Great Coxwell outweigh the social negatives. It is not clear how much information was available to Morris about the actual use of the Great Coxwell barn but subsequent research has revealed that it was a Cistercian business enterprise based on their house at Beaulieu in Hampshire. Lay-brothers and up to fifteen hired servants were employed to do the work. There was tight security at the barn, and the whole of the produce was sold on the open market. It hardly sounds like a progressive business enterprise.[110]

He might also have chosen, as I have chosen, the source of the Thames itself as a destination of symbolic power. But this is disputed territory. Like so many great rivers, the Thames' sources are many. There is no single spot which has the symbolic power which Morris ascribes to the spring in his late novel *The Well at the World's End*, published in the year of his death, 1896. The Thames for Morris, in any case, was never a question of from the source to the sea, but always from one Kelmscott to the other. Morris's life flowed between the weather-beaten stone house across the meadow from the young Thames, near Lechlade, and the brick house which peeps nervously out across the river from behind the flood protection walls at Hammersmith. It is a personal geography, as are all geographies ultimately. The journey in *News from Nowhere* is essentially a journey of the heart, irreducible to theories of art, or society or politics. It is the flowing water which links the key emo-

---

110. The National Trust Oxfordshire, *Great Coxwell Barn*, 1996 leaflet

tional facts of his life — the early infatuation with Jane Burden, the ostler's daughter, in Oxford, their lives together in London and at Kelmscott Manor, their probable infidelities, the busy world of politics and business in London and the private world of self-doubt, desire and failure. It is Morris himself speaking when Ellen says of the 'old house' in chapter thirty-one of *News from Nowhere*:

> "Oh me! Oh me! How I love the earth, and the seasons, and weather, and all things that deal with it, and all that grows out of it, — as this has done!"

Let the great double-bed at the manor stand witness to the many threads which go to make up the fabric of a human life — a seventeenth century oak four-poster with embroidered hangings from the Morris and Co. workshops at Merton. The valance displays the words of Morris's poem 'To the bed at Kelmscott' (1891) embroidered by his daughter May, with possible help from Lily, the daughter of the poet W.B. Yeats. The coverlet was embroidered by Jane Morris and signed with Morris's own motto '*Si je puis*' (If I can). It is worth quoting the complete Morris poem, as it sums up so well Morris's sense of the English countryside, and the emotional frisson of Kelmscott Manor:

> The wind's on the wold and night is a-cold
> And Thames run clear twixt mead and hill
> But kind and dear is the old house here
> And my heart is warm midst winter's harm.
> Rest then and rest and think of the best
> Twixt summer and spring when all birds sing
> In the town of the tree and ye lie in me
> And scarce dare move lest earth and its love
> Should fade away ere the full of the day.
> I am old and have seen many things that have been
> Both grief and peace and wane and increase
> No tale I tell of ill or well
> But this I say: night treadeth on day
> And for worst and best right good is rest.

There is neither self-pity nor self-congratulation here, but a tired man, still in his fifties, coming to terms, as we all must, with success and failure, happiness and sorrow. And death. The water flows continually from source to sea, but for each of us it flows only once. Art, business, politics — the to and fro of Morris's life between one Kelmscott and the other — come to feel like a barrier he erects against the inevitable. Morris is buried at Kelmscott, beneath a tomb designed for him by his old friend Philip Webb. Fiona MacCarthy describes it as having a 'coped roof like a small house or a large dog-kennel.' For her it is 'like an early Frank Lloyd Wright organic building, pushing up out of the soil in its English churchyard setting.'[111] There is none of the cheap symbolism and ornateness of conventional funerary art — the sort that Morris deplored so much in Westminster Abbey. The inscription reads simply WILLIAM MORRIS. The funeral itself appears to have been a tragedy/comedy enacted in appalling wet October weather over a long final haul from Kelmscott House to Kelmscott Manor via Paddington, Oxford and Lechlade. A.R. Dufty, author of the guide to the house, describes the scene at the grey Cotswold town of Lechlade thus:

> The low-lying meadows were flooded and the sound of water was everywhere. Four countrymen in moleskins carried the unpolished oak coffin decorated with a bay wreath to an open haycart with a yellow body and bright red wheels wreathed in vine-leaves, strewn with willow boughs and carpeted with moss.[112]

The life of William Morris may have been a great and glorious epic, but in the end it came down to as much or as little as this.

---

111. MacCarthy, *William Morris*, p.676
112. A.R. Dufty, *Kelmscott: an illustrated guide* (Society of Antiquaries, 1991) p.30

Morris and the myth of the English countryside

Does this pretty little hamlet, tucked away at the end of a by-road leading nowhere, have any significance which is more than personal? I believe it does, for a number of reasons. The Morris 'bed' poem suggests a sense of the English countryside as an unchanging entity which is both factually incorrect and has come to form the basis of a deeply reactionary mythology of rural England. It is part of a larger argument in which so much of what Morris stood for — the crafts, the preservation of ancient buildings, the medieval roots of English culture — has been taken over as part of a heritage industry which threatens to overwhelm the present. The first part of the argument concerns Nature. Now Morris is quite clear on this. He contrasts Iceland, a 'new' country where the landscape is still in the process of formation, and England, which is an 'old' landscape in which the mark of the human hand is ubiquitous. There is no Nature in England, if by Nature we mean wilderness.

In that same famous speech at University College Oxford in 1883,[113] to which I referred in the previous chapter, William Morris made an appeal for careful husbandry of the 'busy lands' that have come to replace Nature, and the conservation of the little remaining wilderness which is all that is left of the original Nature:

> Yet civilization, it seems to me, owes us some compensation for the loss of this romance, which now only hangs like a dream about the country life of busy lands. To keep the air pure and the rivers clean, to take pains to keep the meadows and tillage as pleasant as reasonable use will allow them to be; to allow peaceable citizens freedom to wander where they will, so they do no hurt to garden or cornfield; nay, even to leave here and there some piece of waste or mountain sacredly free from fence or tillage as a memory of man's ruder struggles with nature in his ear-

---

113. Published as William Morris, *Art under plutocracy* (1884)

lier days: is it too much to ask civilization to be so far thoughtful of man's pleasure and rest, and to help as far as this her children to whom she has most often set such heavy tasks of grinding labour? Surely not an unreasonable asking. But not a whit of it shall we get under the present system of society.

Like all myths, the myth of the English countryside, which insistently conflates 'rural' with 'natural' serves a purpose. For Morris, it is used to criticise both industrial, urban squalor and the capitalist system that underpinned modern urbanisation. But for Raymond Williams, in his exhaustive account of country and city as images in English thought, it is capitalism rather than industrialism which is the target:

> (The rural myth) is also a main source for that last protecting illusion in the crisis of our own time: that it is not capitalism which is injuring us, but the more isolable, more evident system of urban industrialism.[114]

Reviewing Williams' book, E.P. Thompson further develops the same idea. For him, this rural myth has become 'softened, protracted, and then taken over by city-dwellers' as part of a general criticism of urban and industrial communities.[115] Instead of the careful husbandry and conservation proposed by Morris, we have 'heritage', which ignores the realities of the countryside today.

The contemporary social thinkers, Ulrich Beck, Anthony Giddens and Scott Lash reach similar conclusions about the 'end of Nature'. 'If human beings once knew what 'nature' was, they do so no longer', they write. 'What is 'natural' is now so thoroughly entangled with what is 'social' that there can be nothing taken for granted about it any more. In common with many aspects of life

---

114. Raymond Williams, *The country and the city* (Oxford University Press, 1973)
115. Reprinted in E.P. Thompson, *Persons and polemics* (Merlin Press, 1994) p.248

governed by tradition, 'nature' becomes transformed into areas of action where human beings have to make practical and ethical decisions.'[116]

Yet for all that, the myth continues. Midway between Morris and our own times, H.V. Morton wrote his bestseller *In Search of England*, the success of which can be gauged by the fact that my own edition, dated 1932, is the seventeenth, just five years after its first appearance. He claims that 'The village that symbolizes England sleeps in the self-consciousness of many a townsman', and that 'the village and the English countryside are the germs of all we are and all we have become.'[117] The realities of the ownership of property and power are concealed, just as 'Eton was slumbering behind elms in well-bred reticence' as he journeyed forth from London. Morton's discovery of the aroma of fish-and-chips at Warrington is a moment of high farce in the book, as is his attempt to explain the 'destiny of the English people' to an American in Peterborough Cathedral. The shadow of Mosley and English fascism is never far away. And of course not only does Morton reject any positive values there might be in industrial England, but he fails utterly to come to terms with the changing countryside.

If we accept that commonly-held views of the rural bear very little correspondence to reality, then we can begin to understand the changes in rural life which took place before, during and after Morris's lifetime. Thomas Hardy, in a preface to *Far from the Madding Crowd*, dated 1895 — 1902, writes of the anachronistic view of 'Wessex' which his early novels promoted:

> ...the press and the public were kind enough to welcome the fanciful plan, and willingly joined me in the anachronism of imagining a Wessex population living under Queen Victoria; — a modern Wessex of railways, the

116. U. Beck, A. Giddens and S. Lash, *Reflexive modernization* (Polity Press, 1994)
117. H.V. Morton, *In search of England* (Methuen, 1927)

penny post, mowing and reaping machines, union work-houses, Lucifer matches, labourers who could read and write, and National School children...

Wessex itself, of course, does not exist. It is another case of heritage playing fast and loose with history, most astonishingly in 1999 when Prince Edward and his bride received the titles of Earl and Countess of Wessex. At least it provided some light relief in the press, with a number of writers pointing out that the previous person to hold the title of Earl of Wessex was Harold, the plucky but unlucky loser of the Battle of Hastings in 1066. Hardy refers to the material changes in the countryside and the cultural results of those changes:

> The change at the root of this has been the recent supplanting of the class of stationary cottagers, who carried on the local traditions and humours, by a population of more or less migratory labourers, which has led to a break of continuity in local history, more fatal than any other thing to the preservation of legend, folklore, close inter-social relations, and eccentric individualities. For these the indispensable conditions of existence are attachment to the soil of one particular spot by generation after generation.

The dislocated lives of Hardy's later characters, Tess and Jude, are examples of a wider social dislocation. It is the very unromantic England which Flora Thompson describes in *Lark Rise to Candleford*. There are plenty of histories, both local and national, in which we can read detailed accounts of the appalling conditions in which rural labourers lived. It is directly reflected at the end of *News from Nowhere*, in the ragged figure Guest sees upon awakening, who contrasts with the 'joyous beautiful people' he has just left at the harvest feast in Kelmscott church:

> His face was rugged, and grimed rather than dirty; his eyes dull and bleared; his body bent, his calves thin and

spindly, his feet dragging and limping. His clothing was a mixture of dirt and rags long over-familiar to me. As I passed him he touched his hat with some real goodwill and courtesy, and much servility.

But of course there was resistance to these processes. The Swing riots of the 1830s led in particular to attacks on the new farm machinery which was making many rural labourers redundant. The Tolpuddle Martyrs were deported to Australia for attempting to form a trade union in their little Dorset village. Farm labourers continued to organise, however, particularly in Joseph Arch's National Agricultural Labourers' Union in the early 1870s. I am grateful to Alan Tuckett, director of the National Institute of Adult Continuing Education, for the following story, which ties us nicely back into the work of William Morris:

> "One of the most active branches of William Morris's Socialist League was in Norwich. On Sunday mornings they would go out and harangue the populace of a small village called Horsham St Faiths. They did this for about two years and then it petered out, in the way of lots of progressive social initiatives. And seemingly nothing happened, there were no obvious outcomes, the whole thing was a waste of time really. Seven years later, it was in Horsham St Faiths that the National Union of Agricultural Workers was founded after one hundred years of attempts to create a general workers' union for agricultural workers."

Yet here we are, one hundred years later, still talking about 'the rural' as if it means anything at all. Well, does it? We can begin by looking at where people live and the way they earn their living. Now it is true that in some parts of Europe — I am thinking in particular of parts of southern and eastern Europe — there are communities where most people earn their living from agriculture. Depopulation is still a problem in some of these areas. In England, by contrast, so-called 'rural' populations have been increasing in virtually every part of the country since the 1960s. Ironically this has been largely as a result of the extension of private car ownership which occurred at the same historical moment as the government decided to close so many rural branchlines of the railway system, marking the victory of the roads lobby over the public transport lobby. Now it is the great industrial towns which are losing population. It is not just a question of suburban London spreading its tentacles ever further into the countryside. Counties such as North Yorkshire and Norfolk are increasing in population at the same rate as East Sussex. Cornwall, that county-nation outpost of the Celtic world, bastion of low pay, surfing and out-migration of its young people, is building up its population more swiftly still — mainly in the form of retirement pensioners.

Yet if the division between rural and urban seems more tenuous than it used to, there are serious problems in the countryside. Some of the worst aspects of rural life which Ebenezer Howard described in his *Garden Cities of Tomorrow*[118] — isolation and poor services — persist. But they persist because of poverty. As more and more relatively well off people move into the countryside, as bus services become less frequent, more expensive and less dependable, as local village shops close because 'most people' (the new countrysiders) prefer to shop in the supermarket in the nearest town, so the position of those who are short of jobs and money and cars becomes worse. The poverty is hidden, hidden behind that unreal picture-postcard, calendar, birthday card image of England which stands defiantly against otherness. In the cities the others are defined by the colour of their skins or the nature of their sexuality. In the countryside they are often the very people who have most roots in the countryside, plus the children of those for whom the idyll of rural bliss has broken down in an age of insecure employment, redundancy and family breakdown.

---

118. Ebenezer Howard, *Garden cities of tomorrow* (1902, new revised edition with introduction by Ray Thomas, Attic, 1985)

The nature of agricultural work itself has changed. Farmers now refer to the 'agriculture industry' and use the common business parlance of investment, return and maximising profit. As with all business, agriculture is not required to account for social costs. We are now beginning to realise that these social costs exist: contamination of ground-water supplies by artificial fertilisers and pesticides, reductions in biodiversity through monocropping, and animal infections such as BSE. The reference to the latter as Mad Cow Disease is part of the problem: if at one level we refuse to confront the realities of what is happening in the English countryside, at another the media becomes dominated by panic reactions which sweep the country and disappear, to leave very little unchanged. Who now remembers the scares of the late '80s about salmonella in eggs? Yet it is still there, and poultry-farming methods have changed little in the intervening years. The 'crisis' of English agriculture is not just about declining farm incomes, but also the refusal of many in the agricultural industry to face the facts that 'modern' farming methods are poisoning the land.

There is a need for dialogue in the English countryside. Dialogue about farming methods between organic and non-organic farmers, with other European countries about the Common Agricultural Policy and how this could be used to promote sustainable rather than destructive farming methods. Dialogue too about jobs. Any plan to set up a business or install a factory, however clean and neat and tidy, is met with the 'assumption against development' which dominates planing regulations in rural areas. 'Not in My Back Yard' is a knee-jerk reaction with official backing. A third area that would benefit from dialogue is transport, with a need to work out new and imaginative ways of providing public transport in rural areas. Remote parts of Britain are already used to this with their post-minibuses that combine mail collection and delivery with passenger services. Swiss railways offer a special 'rover' ticket that includes both ferries and post-buses! There is scope too to call on the voluntary effort of relatively well-off incomers to rural areas to provide car-lifts to hospital appointments and on shopping trips for other residents. In many cases, subsidised taxis will be a better and cheaper way of increasing mobility for the rural poor than the option of a daily bus service which may or may not leave at a convenient time or follow a convenient route. A village can only be a community when there is dialogue between all its members on the key material issues of housing, jobs and health, as well as over the prettifying of village gardens, the stewardship of heritage and the organisation of cultural events.

Kelmscott: the village and the Manor

It is instructive in this sense to see what has happened to Kelmscott itself. The village lies in the corner of Oxfordshire, two and a half miles from Lechlade. Gloucestershire and Berkshire are both within sight, Wiltshire is less than two miles away. There is no public transport. As the Society of Antiquaries, the current owners of the house, have bowed to pressure to make the house more available to Morris enthusiasts, so the pressure on the village has increased, with cars and coaches fighting for space in the narrow lanes around the village. The Morris family did at least make some investment in the village with a pair of memorial cottages erected by Jane Morris in 1902 and designed by Philip Webb, and some later cottages built in 1915 by May Morris to designs by the Cotswold Arts and Crafts architect, Ernest Gimson. There is also the village hall — the Morris Memorial Hall — which provides a focus for village activities. It was opened in 1934 by George Bernard Shaw. Also present was the National Coalition Prime Minister, Ramsay MacDonald, who as a young man had been a member of Morris's Social Democratic Federation. The village also boasts a pub, the Plough, which augments its local trade with income from visitors to the

Manor. A tennis court was paid for out of the 1953 Coronation collection, but has gone. The village shop has closed. The elms have gone too, victims of the terrible scourge of Dutch elm disease.

The later history of Kelmscott Manor is also an interesting tale. Of William Morris's daughters, Jenny suffered throughout her life from epilepsy and depended very much on the affection and support of her father. His letters to her are among the most distinctive of his enormous output; tender, domestic, yet also connecting her to the wider world of art, politics and business in which Morris himself moved. She was devastated by his death and as Fiona MacCarthy writes: 'He had been not just her father but her main companion and in a sense her last real link with the outside world.'[119] She lived on until 1935 in a twilight world of companions and nursing homes.

May Morris, by contrast, devoted herself to the Morris inheritance, founding the Women's Guild of Art in 1907 and completing the mammoth task of editing the *Complete Works* in 1915. In 1926 she turned to the question of the future of Kelmscott Manor, which her mother had purchased shortly before her death in 1914. Much of the drama of the Kelmscott legacy pivots around the terms under which May Morris bequeathed the house to the University of Oxford. However, the terms of the covenant made it extremely difficult for the University to finance the upkeep of Kelmscott. The house was cold, damp and draughty, with a water supply from a polluted well. The University found it impossible to find tenants for the house prepared to pay the kind of rent which would cover the costs of maintaining it. Faced with a situation in which their ownership of Kelmscott Manor was being subsidised out of general University funds, the University had the covenant declared invalid and passed the house and its contents to the residuary legatee, the Society of Antiquar-

119. MacCarthy, *William Morris*, p.678

ies, in 1960. The writ was served politely over lunch in an Oxford college.

Peter Locke, the young architect at Donald Insall Associates directly responsible for the work of restoration, had been one of the first post-war Lethaby scholars of the Society for the Protection of Ancient Buildings, established by Morris himself in 1877. In an interview in 1996, Locke emphasised how his practice stemmed directly from Morris's principles. Firstly that buildings, like people, need proper 'looking after', with daily care and maintenance. Secondly that where maintenance fails, repairs should be on the basis of 'minimum intervention'. Thirdly that buildings are functional objects which may need alteration if they cannot fulfil their function, and that such changes should be made in a contemporary style. We talked about Cambridge and its exciting blend of high quality architecture from late mediaeval to high modern, with buildings in disparate styles often cheek by jowl.

Locke emphasised that May Morris was going against her father's own precepts in refusing to allow change or repair to the house both during her lifetime and in her will: "instead of preserving it, she was hastening its destruction." He contrasted this with Morris himself, one of whose last acts at Kelmscott was to lift damp flag-stones and have them replaced by a wooden floor. The job was a nightmare with fresh problems at every turn: Locke described how he and 'Dick' Dufty, author of the official guide to Kelmscott, used to go into Faringdon in the afternoon to have tea and "hold one another up". At the same time, he found loyal support in the long-standing Burford building firm employed to do the job. Unlike the craftsmen employed to build the steps to the John F. Kennedy memorial, mentioned in chapter three, he needed no patronising references to football crowds to inspire the workers! He remembers the following exchange:

> "Be careful not to clean up the roof slates and keep the moss on."
> "Oh well, we always do, Mr Locke!"

Kelmscott Manor as we see it today is a tribute to the notions of conservation passed down from Morris himself, the craftsmanship of the English building workers and the careful and principled management of the Society of Antiquaries. On a visit I made there in the wet and stormy June of 1997, the ground around the house was strewn with evidence of the concerns of Peter Locke and the Cotswold building workers: the glistening green-black clumps of moss beaten from the slates by the tropical overnight rain onto the paving slabs with ripening alpine strawberries between them. But there was also plenty left to contrast in its luminous sheen with the underlying greyness of the hand-cut slates and the yellow-green lichen coating their surfaces. It is much as Heather Tanner described the living nature of Oolitic limestone in *Wiltshire Village* in the 1930s: 'When it is old and grey it is alive with new growth — emerald moss, orange spots of lichen, stonecrop and rue-leaved saxifrage, pennycress and cobwebbed ivy'.[120]

There was the mulberry tree as well, now too old to stand without supporting props, more gnarled than I had remembered on a previous visit when my attention was first drawn to it by a notice saying 'Please do not walk under the mulberry tree.' Apart from the unlikely misfortune of a bough breaking under the weight of the ripe September fruit, the main concern of the staff was that the bright red juice of the fallen mulberries might get tramped into the house by visitors and spoil the delicate faded colours of the Morris carpets. Over a century old, this tree is a direct connection with Morris as you gaze out of the bedroom window towards the herbaceous borders, the willows and the river. A young tree has been planted as an eventual replacement. The Nature of birth, growth, reproduction and death is implacable, as it is in Morris's poem 'November' from *The Earthly Paradise*, when the narra-

---

120. H. Heather Tanner, *Wiltshire village* (1939, reprinted Impact Books, 1987)

tor, urged to turn away from his misery towards the 'real world' sees only this:

> Yea, I have looked and seen November there;
> The changeless seal of change it seemed to be,
> Fair death of things that, living once, were fair;
> Bright sign of loneliness too great for me,
> Strange image of the dread eternity,
> In whose void patience how can these have part,
> These outstretched feverish hands, this restless heart?

But to return to my June 1997 visit: the main road along the north bank of the Thames from Radcot Bridge to Lechlade passes through a pleasant countryside of corn-fields and hedges with damp hills in the distance. The turning to Kelmscott is a single-track road which winds through the village before eventually rejoining the larger road before Lechlade. The closer to the Thames I draw, the wetter it is, with deep ditches bordering the road and layer upon layer of rain-clouds gathering high above the water-meadows. England is patterned in the richest shades of green and white — cow-parsley, elderflower, hog-weed, moon-daisies, white campion — and puddles which reflect the translucent, silver sky. It is Ladies' Day at Ascot and the rain falls.

Within the village, a single turning leads down to Kelmscott Manor and its car-park and peters out just round the corner among the dog-roses and willows on the banks of the Thames. The Manor boasts a shop where the Morris heritage industry is in full swing. There are waste-paper baskets, tea-caddies, oven-gloves, postcards, paper, tiles, all in traditional Morris patterns. I remembered Peter Locke saying to me that not only were Morris designs ubiquitous in middle-class English homes, but that these objects were probably the only ones the owner could point to and identify the designer. I bought a tea-towel of the frontispiece of *News from Nowhere* and a pot of local honey, thinking that they might turn out to be both beautiful and useful. But these signs of the heritage industry at work cannot obscure the real excitement that any lover of Morris and his work feels on coming to Kelmscott. As John Kay of the William Morris Society described it:

> My wife and I first came here on a golden July evening in 1955. We walked up the lane from the river, where we had moored the small boat that had brought us from London — as Guest and Ellen do in *News from Nowhere*. As yet unrestored, the Manor looked agreeably lived in, if a bit shabby, in the evening light. The great elms still stood in the hedgerows.[121]

Yet Kelmscott is a working village too, with farmhouses, cottages and some plain 1950s council houses straggling along the length of its single road. A poster in one small cottage window invites people to attend the Countryside Rally in Hyde Park, London on 10 July 1997 — 'Life in the countryside may never be the same again'. The 'threat' was the possibility that the newly elected Labour government might support a private member's bill in Parliament to ban hunting. Yet there is no sign in the village of opposition to the constant intrusion into village life of enormous transport planes grumbling and groaning in and out of the United States Air Force base at Fairford, a key base for NATO action against the Iraqi invasion of Kuwait and against Serb actions in both Bosnia and Kosovo during the 1990s. Indeed, the main danger to these pretty Cotswold villages is that of becoming 'second home ghettos' as house prices increasingly favour incomers over locals who cannot afford the prices.

The village has a post-box and a pub, The Plough, which does bed-and-breakfast, but no post office, shop or school. A mobile library calls on alternate Thursdays. Its only apparent amenity, apart from the pub, is the Village Hall. By chance, my visit coincided with the arrival of two people to set up a weekend textiles workshop run by the District Council and Southern Arts. The tutor Sally MacCabe

---

121. John Kay, *'News from nowhere' and the English countryside*

explained to me that she had also been involved in a William Morris Society event which had been set up as a community project:[122]

> "...it was involving people in the craft of textiles who were not (experts). And we had about five people local from the village and then some people from local quilt groups as well came. And then there were (four) schools involved with projects. They made quilts and really did some amazing work. Three primary, one secondary, the secondary was Burford, the primary was one in Witney and a small one which is the local one for this village, Langford... and one in Lechlade, St Clothilde's."

She explained that children and parents worked together during the holidays, collecting images of natural life and then turning it into quilting with spray painting, before adding:

> "The workshop tomorrow is with adults, most of whom have got experience and a strong interest in textiles, some belong to the Embroidery group in Oxford, I've got a lady coming from Tokyo, she comes over every year... We're looking at images of flowers, botanical themes from the (Kelmscott Manor) garden but treating them in a contemporary way with stitch and silk painting."

There is, of course, a certain editing of history in this linking of Morris with the contemporary crafts movement in the Cotswolds. In a *New Statesman* article, Paul Barker linked it more directly to C.R. Ashbee's decision to move his Guild of Handicraft to Chipping Campden in the Cotswolds from Whitechapel in 1902. Despite Ashbee's own subsequent sense of failure, the move to the Cotswolds lit a slow-burning fuse which flickers still. As Paul Barker comments:

---

122. This project is mentioned in *'News from nowhere' and the English countryside*, and in more detail in *Embroidery in Kelmscott: a community arts project in West Oxfordshire led by Sue Rangeley* (William Morris Society, 1991)

Like many supposed failures, it had powerful lines of descent. You can trace back to this rural dottiness the origins of the conservation movement, the Land is Ours campaign, even (via Edward Carpenter) gay rights. And the crafts, once begun, continued...The Gloucestershire Guild of Craftsmen holds its annual show in August at Painswick, near Stroud, in a building decorated with carvings by Eric Gill, under Ashbee's influence.[123]

At Campden itself, the Silk Mill to which the guildsmen came in 1902 houses not only a permanent exhibition about the Guild, but also the workshops of a number of contemporary craftspeople. One of them, the silversmith David Hart, is the grandson of one of the original guildsmen, and the family line looks sets to continue. He employs a son and nephew as well as another local school-leaver in the workshop.

The children: a future for the English countryside?

On my watery visit to Kelmscott in June 1997, there was no indication on the notice-board outside the hall of a regular programme of locally-based events, although the hall is affiliated to the Oxford Rural Community Council. An advertisement on a telegraph-pole for a fund-raising event caught my eye. It belonged to a pre-school and I remembered that I had seen a woman earlier in the afternoon in Kelmscott wearing a T-shirt advertising this particular pre-school at Broadwell, a neighbouring village. It was a further two years before I followed up this lead, and visited Broadwell itself. On the last day of an equally wet June, I went to visit Jackie Overton to find out more about the Broadshires pre-school. They use an attractive little stone building more or less opposite the local pub, the Five Bells. The building used to be the village school and is now

---

123. Paul Barker, *New Statesman*, 20/6/97

owned and run by a village trust, with the pre-school as the main users. The Trust have redecorated the hall and repaired the roof, while the pre-school pay rent and heating and electricity bills. Jackie and her assistant both live in Kelmscott and try to make sure that priority is given to children from the villages. They are helped by a few mobile parents from Lechlade and Carterton (the 'town' attached to the Brize Norton airforce base) who bring their children along to Broadwell. It is a sensible arrangement which suits both village and town people — the kind of arrangement which helps to sustain rural activities in a number of fields by encouraging mobile townspeople to travel out to activities in the villages, rather than in the more usual opposite direction.

With the new emphasis placed by the Labour Government on pre-school education, there have been some improvements. The pre-school is free to children over four, and it is hoped that this public subsidy will eventually be extended to the over threes as well. These younger children were being charged £3.25 per session in 1999. The income helps to purchase equipment, pay the rent and pay the staff, although parents still provide additional voluntary help. Rural activities of this sort, which are often taken for granted in towns and cities, still need plenty of friends though. The group's most recent fund-raising event, a car-boot sale, raised £857. However, there are drawbacks to state support. The pre-school has to work to nationally set targets for children's learning, (as if children of this age needed any encouragement to learn), and are inspected by government inspectors, the dreaded and despised Office for Standards in Education. The intuitive approach to learning which has always characterised the pre-school movement, in which children learn by playing and doing, is fast being replaced by a more systematic approach which is in danger of obscuring the joy which young children find in learning. But Jackie clings to the idea that 'choice' must be a central organising principle and is glad to find that co-operation, children sharing and caring in the context of play, is recognised as a 'desirable outcome' of pre-school.

The primary school at nearby Langford is growing rapidly. A decade ago it was threatened by closure because of its falling rolls, but from fifty-six children in 1992 has grown to one hundred. Langford, too, has William Morris connections. It was one of the schools in Oxfordshire which came under the spell of Robin Tanner, engraver, and rather unlikely Her Majesty's Inspector of Schools in the 1960s. Indeed Tanner observed that under the Welsh headteacher David Evans, 'the work done by the Langford boys and girls has never been exceeded anywhere.'[124] Tanner and the teachers like David Evans at Langford who worked alongside him in the classroom and on courses, inspired a previous generation of Oxfordshire children to produce creative designs in a number of craft media. Tanner describes this work in his autobiographical *Double Harness*, published in 1987, a year before his death. His career is a useful reminder that the discourse of education has not always been that of a shrunken and uninspiring National Curriculum. As he observed in *Double Harness*:

> The great immeasurable qualities of feeling, of personal creativity, of discrimination, of sensitive awareness of others, and of dedicated service seemed more and more to be regarded as lesser by-products commendable but unimportant.[125]

I think he would have approved of the Broadwell pre-school with its happy, healthy children playing imaginative games with hoops in the garden in the June sunshine. It is precisely the definition of education that Morris himself used in *How we live and how we might live*:

> And you must not say that every English child is educated now; that sort of education will not answer my claim,

124. Robin Tanner, *Double harness*, p.162
125. R. Tanner, p.150

though I cheerfully admit it is something; something, and yet after all only class education. What I claim is Liberal education; opportunity, that is, to have my share of whatever knowledge there is in the world according to my capacity or bent of mind, historical or scientific; and also to have my share of skill of hand which is about in the world, either in the industrial handicrafts or in the fine arts...

In his later years, Tanner felt that Mrs Thatcher had turned back the clock on many of the developments with which he had been associated. He wrote: 'It was a terrible tragedy, not only for education but for the whole of English life .' And a little further on: 'Our country was daily becoming a crueller, meaner, duller, uglier place in which to live.'[126] Yet he also uses lines from Morris's *Dream of John Ball* to suggest the continuity and the moral value of the struggle for democratic, humane values.

It is in looking at issues related to children — how we care for them, how we educate them — that the shortcomings of the heritage approach to the English countryside become most obvious. Children and their parents need practical support such as affordable childcare and good local schools with a varied and stimulating curriculum. They need, too, the little gains that can come from people looking creatively at the problems of their local community. For example, in Kelmscott the local community has recently been given the use of a field as a play area where football posts can be erected. Jackie Overton's two boys are delighted, although the villagers themselves will have to put up the posts. Eventually those boys will need jobs, and the promotion of small-scale, non-polluting employment in the countryside is of great importance to the liveliness of these rural communities of the upper Thames. It is extremely unlikely that any of these new enterprises will damage the countryside as much as large-scale, publicly subsidised, indus-

---

126. R. Tanner, p.186

trialised agriculture is doing. Finally, there is culture, a question of offering children access to the traditional arts and crafts but in ways which allow their own creative spirits to blossom, no more and no less than they blossom to the sounds of the international pop culture which they share in too.

Just across the river lies Buscot Park, an extensive National Trust property which houses the Faringdon collection of paintings. It is unusual for a National Trust 'stately home' in that the residents, Lord Faringdon and his family, are still adding to the art collection, and still adding fresh attractions to the gardens outside. It is also unusual in having played a significant role in left-wing politics under Gavin Henderson, the second Lord Faringdon. In the 1930s he supported the Spanish Republic, and as a convinced pacifist, he served with the Fire Brigade in London and Bristol during the Second World War. He served on the committee of the Fabian Society and as a London County Councillor in the 1960s. Political weekend parties were a frequent occurrence at Buscot, with Nye Bevan, father of the National Health Service, a frequent and popular visitor. Some murals tucked away in the grounds near the swimming-pool depict scenes from this political life of Buscot, including the banner of the Faringdon Labour Party.

In 1891, the first Lord Faringdon had purchased the four large pictures illustrating the story of the Sleeping Beauty (the 'Legend of the Briar Rose' to give it its more formal title), which Burne-Jones had been working on in various forms since 1871, for the saloon at Buscot Park. While staying with his friend William Morris across at Kelmscott Manor, Burne-Jones visited Buscot and decided on new settings for the pictures, linked by panels continuing the rose and weaving motifs, which were eventually completed in 1895. Recently restored, the paintings are stunning in their impact. The story is told in words (by Morris himself) around the room, with each set of four lines referring to a major panel:

The fateful slumber floats and flows
About the tangle of the rose.
But lo the fated hand and heart
To rend the slumberous curse apart.
    The threat of war, the hope of peace,
    The kingdom's peril and increase.
    Sleep on and bide the latter day
    When fate shall take her chains away.
The maiden pleasance of the land
Knoweth no stir of voice or hand,
No cup the sleeping waters fill,
The restless shuttle lieth still.
    Here lies the hoarded love, the key
    To all the treasure that shall be.
    Come, fated hand, the gift to take
    And smite the sleeping world awake.

It is hard not to read into these lines the plea for hope, courage and renewal that Morris makes consistently in his social and political writings. Heritage looks backwards not forwards. It tells us where we have come from, but not in an unambiguous form from which we can read off directions about which way to travel in the future. Authentic identity must encompass past, present and future. We need to know what our English culture has been, including its conflicts, silences and omissions. We need to recognise how poor and constrained our lives together have become. As Morris wrote over a century ago:

> I feel sure that the time will come when men and women will find it difficult to believe that such a rich community as ours, having such command over external Nature, could ever have submitted to live such a mean shabby, dirty, ugly life as we do now! (*How we live and how we might live*)

Chapter 10
Life, the universe and everything:
a trip to the source of the Thames

And I have felt
A presence that disturbs me with the joy
Of elevated thoughts; a sense sublime
Of something far more deeply interfused,
Whose dwelling is the light of setting suns,
And the round ocean and the living air,
And the blue sky, and in the mind of man;
A motion and a spirit, that impels
All thinking things, all objects of all thought,
And rolls through all things.
(William Wordsworth, 'Lines composed a few miles above
Tintern Abbey', 1798)

There was this Englishman who worked in the London
office of a multinational corporation based in the United
States. He drove home one evening in his Japanese car.
His wife, who worked in a firm which imported German
kitchen equipment, was already at home. Her small Italian car was often quicker through the traffic. After a meal
which included New Zealand lamb, Californian carrots,
Mexican honey, French cheese and Spanish wine, they
settled down to watch a programme on their television
set, which had been made in Finland. The programme was
a retrospective celebration of the war to recapture the
Falkland Islands. As they watched it they felt warmly
patriotic, and proud to be British. (Raymond Williams)[127]

Sources

Anticipating the millennium by nearly twenty years, Raymond Williams wrote of the confused nature of national

---

127. Raymond Williams, 'The culture of nations', in *Towards 2000,*
    p.177

and cultural identity in a world of economic and cultural relations increasingly organised at the global level. Utopia for Morris was a real place — England. But England is a confusing place, a cross-roads, in which nothing is what it seems and everything has the power to transmogrify into something else. Thomas Hardy saw this, and more, looking back on the Dorset of the 1840s, and describing bonfire night on Egdon Heath in *The Return of the Native*:

> It was as if these men and boys had suddenly dived into past ages, and fetched therefrom an hour and deed which had before been familiar with this spot. The ashes of the original British pyre which blazed from that summit lay fresh and undisturbed in the barrow beneath their tread. The flames from funeral piles long ago kindled there had shone down upon the lowlands as these were shining now. Festival fires to Thor and Woden had followed on the same ground and duly had their day. Indeed, it is pretty well known that such blazes as this the heathmen were now enjoying are rather the lineal descendants from jumbled druidical rites and Saxon ceremonies than the invention of popular feeling about Gunpowder Plot.[128]

Hardy also points to the persistent habit of fundamental issues (about the nature and purpose of human life) cutting across the accidents of time and place:

> Moreover to light a fire is the instinctive and resistant act of man when, at the winter ingress, the curfew is sounded throughout Nature. It indicates a spontaneous, Promethean rebelliousness against the fiat that this recurrent season shall bring foul times, cold darkness, misery and death. Black chaos comes, and the fettered gods of the earth say, Let there be light.[129]

In our failure to find Utopia anywhere up the Thames from London to Kelmscott, in our awareness of the

---

128. Thomas Hardy, *The return of the native* (1880, reprinted The Folio Society, 1971), pp.32-33
129. Hardy, *The return of the native*, p.33

dystopia of so much of modern life, we are left with the source of the Thames. *Nowhere* is a hole in a field somewhere in Gloucestershire. Patrick Wright has written hilariously of the sudden obsession in the 1980 with 'mineral water' — in a Britain in which 'the hills were suddenly alive with the sound of water running into plastic bottles.'[130] If you don't believe this, please go the Malvern Hills any weekend and listen to it happening. Wright sees us recreating our origins in the obscure corners, frequently quaintly named, from which we extract our precious bottled water. The only move he missed was the feasibility study to market Slough water in 1990 — from what is supposed to be a ten thousand year old spring.[131] At the same time, and more seriously, the new cult reflects the lack of confidence in a viable public sphere, the linking of heritage and identity to social progress in a very English and modest form of modernity. It is a line that begins confidently enough with William Morris and George Lansbury, with the garden cities and the early days of municipal housing and public health, but which trickles to an uncertain stop in the failure of the Welfare State to provide more than a safety net for the most needy in our society. Wright shows an acute sense of both cultural and political history when he concludes:

> Bottled Britain asserts the traditional geography of the nation against the placeless world of the statutory public supply where uniformity and standardization are now more associated with poison than, as they certainly were in the age of cholera, with the hard-won guarantee of public health.[132]

As Wright notes, there is a dangerous solemnity about talk of sources, in which Morris himself shared. In Morris's

130. Patrick Wright, *A journey through ruins*, pp.222-3
131. Michael Cassell, *Long lease! The story of Slough Estates*
132. Patrick Wright, *A journey through ruins*, p.223

romance *The Well at the World's End*, Ralph and Ursula eventually reach and drink from a magic well by the sea-side, which heals their wounds and gives them courage to face the challenges of the rest of their lives. They would have a harder time with the Thames. There is no real agreement about the source of the Thames, as was made clear to me on my first expedition to find the source of the Thames, by a photographer in the car-park of the Thames Head Inn on the ancient Fosseway route between Tetbury and Cirencester. He tells me that of course the true 'source' is Seven Springs, near Cheltenham, the springs that feed the larger tributary, the Churn, which flows down through Cirencester to meet the Thames at Crick-lade, on the eastern fringe of the Cotswold Water Park. Even the name is controversial — the 'Thames or Isis' on our map. The only other river I know which bears a dual name on the OS map is the 'Piddle or Trent' in Dorset, renamed when Queen Victoria found the name of the river and its associated villages offensive.

Well, it has to be said that this source of the Thames is not a mountain stream, a great glacier, water springing from hard rock, but a damp hole in a field in Gloucester-shire. After following a line of field maples through a herd of grazing heifers, after crossing the Great Western Rail-way's Swindon-Gloucester line, after making our way through a disused goods yards with a couple of abandoned road tankers. Interesting? Yes. Bucolic? Most certainly not. It also has to be said that the dampness owed more to the effects of a remarkably wet winter than to the pres-ence of an actual spring. It is a state of affairs that has per-sisted for a very long while. Runciman, in his 1885 book about the Thames, *Royal River*, describes it thus in May, over one hundred years before my visit:

> The sweet-smelling grass is spangled with daisies and but-tercups, though not so profusely as in the field adjacent, which is destined for a crop of hay; and the grove resounds with bird-music set in the rapturous key of the bridal sea-

son. And there, a few paces athwart the sward, under the shadow of trembling foliage, is the spot which for centuries was said to be the birthplace of the Thames. We are at Thames Head, in Trewsbury Mead, in the parish of Cotes, in the county of Gloucestershire, three miles south-west of Cirencester.[133]

Runciman puts down the lack of water to the activities of the 'ugly pump-house' taking water for the nearby Thames and Severn canal. He notes that there are other obvious springs in the area. This theme of the impact of human activity on the basic water supply in the area has come down from Morris's days to our own. The canal is now a boggy, rural rubbish tip, but the activities of quarries and gravel pits, plus the increased domestic consumption of water, have all further impacted on the springs in the area. Early in 1997 this state of affairs even drew the attention of the popular press with an article in the *Evening Standard* under the headline 'A journey down dry old Father Thames.' In an inconclusive article, the journalists concerned put the lack of water in the Thames down variously to increased water extraction and the very dry period in Southern England in the mid-'90s.[134]

While Runciman's bird-song is present in the form of a woodpecker noisily repairing its nesting hole in the giant ash-tree that stands guard over the most famous hole in the ground in England, there are new noises too. There is the distant hum of a circling light aircraft, the clatter of resurfacing work across the fields on the A433 (the Fosse Way); a busy but rather elderly two-car diesel train running into Kemble. Below the ash-tree and the woodpecker stands a plaque, identifying this spot as indeed the historic source of the Thames. It was erected in 1974 by the Conservators of the River Thames when the statues of Old

---

133. J. Runciman, *The royal river: the Thames from source to sea* (1885, reprinted Bloomsbury Books, 1993)
134. 'A journey down dry old Father Thames', *Evening Standard*, 4 April 1997

Father Thames was moved to St John's lock in Lechlade, the last and highest on the river. The statue makes a nice composition with the busy river scene, the quiet water meadows, and the spire of Lechlade church standing sentry over the upper Thames. And Old Father Thames is still depicted on the gable of the Thames Head Inn on the Fosse Way where the Arkell's bitter is decidedly more bucolic than the infant Thames.

Water: the material, the spiritual and the political

In the end, the source of the Thames matters for three intertwined reasons; one material; the second symbolic and spiritual; and the third political. As we saw above, the protagonists in *The Well at the World's End* seek for understanding and healing at a remote well. Yet understanding and healing can only begin with self-knowledge and self-love. There is ample evidence in Morris that suggests that water was a much more everyday experience. It was part of the closely woven fabric of his daily activities, and the sense that his own life made to him as joy in its everyday details and activities. Read, for example, his letters to his younger daughter, which are full of this complex texture of the changing seasons, the humdrum, the romance of the ordinary and the repeated. Or the letter he wrote on 24 December 1884 to Georgiana Burne-Jones, on his return from a visit to Edward Carpenter's little commune near Sheffield, from which I have already quoted in chapter five. In this letter he contrasts the 'mean squabbles' of the Social Democratic Federation with the simple joys of Carpenter's gay Arcadia: *'the real way to enjoy life is to accept all its necessary ordinary details'*.

Florence Boos, an American academic who has been at the forefront of attempts to insist on the continuing relevance of Morris to the modern world, has distinguished between what she calls a 'bucolic' Morris and a 'political' Morris. The following quote from 'The prospects of architecture in civilisation' (1881) is taken as paradigmatic of the 'bucolic' Morris:

> For we indeed freed from the bondage of foolish habit and dulling luxury might at last have eyes wherewith to see: and should have to babble to one another many things of our joy in the life around us: the faces of people in the streets bearing the tokens of mirth and sorrow and hope, and all the tale of their lives: the scraps of nature the busiest of us would come across; birds and beasts and the little worlds they live in; and even in the very town the sky above us and the drift of the clouds across it; the wind's hand on the slim trees, and its voice amid their branches, and all the ever-recurring deeds of nature: nor would the road or the river winding past our homes fail to tell us stories of the country-side, and men's doings in field and fell.[135]

The glorious reality for Morris is not an abstracted 'nature' detached from people or their lives but the nature of town and country, permeated by the work and agency of human kind. Indeed, this is the point of the essay, which is about architecture, vernacular architecture in particular and Broadway especially, seeing it as a place where buildings grow from natural resources and add to the beauty of the world rather than detracting from it. In Morris's words: 'this simple harmless beauty that was no hindrance or trouble to any man, and that added to the natural beauty of the earth instead of marring it'.

So I would argue that the 'bucolic' in Morris, rather than somehow contrasting with his 'political' views, is central to his political thought. That is if we take political in its broadest sense of how human affairs can be organised to create harmony between one person and the next, and between human beings and their environment. It is a question of

---

135. Florence Boos, 'An aesthetic ecocommunist: Morris the red and Morris the green', in (eds) P. Faulkner and P. Preston, *William Morris centenary essays*, papers from the Morris Centenary Conference organised by the William Morris Society at Exeter College Oxford, 30 June-3 July 1996 (University of Exeter Press, 1999) pp.21-46

giving due weight to Morris's immediate perceptions of the essential harmony between people and their environment. It is an everyday version of Wordsworth's 'sense sublime'. It is Morris fishing at Kelmscott rather than worrying about the origins of the Thames. It is me finding a bathing hole, over-hung by ash and willow, in a meander of the infant Thames at Somerford Keynes, with a gravel beach and a deep pit which the current has gouged from the bank. A dried cow-pat floats serenely past, tiny blue dragonflies hover above the surface. There are willows, ashes, reeds and bird-song and excited dogs chasing after sticks. A little upstream there is the heady scent of elderflower and dog-roses. In the water are yellow flags and broad patches of water crowfoot raising their simple white heads on slim elegant stems above the slow-moving water.

I am indebted to Theodore Roszak[136] for reminding me of the pertinence of Wordsworth's often quoted lines in his Tintern Abbey poem, to my argument here. It is most evi-dently in our harmonious relationship with nature that we intuit the sense of our own lives, while leaving open the question of a possible overall sense and shape in the uni-verse we inhabit. In a nutshell, the universe is meaningful for people if we will open our minds to it, but whether we are meaningful to the universe is quite another matter. What Roszak misses, and Morris captures in *News from Nowhere*, is the ethical platform of environmentalism. Just before the lines quoted above, Wordsworth wrote of

...that best portion of a good man's life,
His little, nameless, unremembered, acts
Of kindness and of love.

It is, I suspect, a sentiment that Morris would have shared. And certainly one that would have appealed to the progressive instincts of Tolstoy or the kindly anarchism of Kropotkin, who wrote:

---

136. Theodore Roszak, *The voice of the earth* (Bantam, 1993)

It is not love and not even sympathy upon which society is based in mankind. It is the conscience — be it only at the stage of an instinct — of human solidarity. It is the unconscious recognition of the force that is borrowed by each man from the practice of mutual aid; of the close dependency of everyone's happiness upon the happiness of all; and of the sense of justice, or equity, which brings the individual to consider the rights of every other individual as equal to his own. Upon this broad and necessary foundation the still higher moral feelings are developed.[137]

For all that Morris read Marx and called himself a communist, it is the communitarian strand of nineteenth century thinking that his lyricism most strongly brings to mind.

But Morris, as I have insisted at various points in this book, is a call to action rather than a call to contemplation. Water may stand as a symbol of wisdom and understanding but its purity and its availability in human culture is of fundamental material importance. In Southern England 'water problems' mean a ban on sprinklers and hosepipes. On a global basis, such problems mean that nearly two billion people do not have a safe, clean water supply. Without even beginning to address the ethical issues around the privatisation of water supplies and their co-option as a source of profit, there are water issues throughout the Thames valley. A list would include the impact on the water table of over-extraction for domestic and industrial purposes; the sheer amount of water used by individuals and industries; the actual and potential pollution of underground water supplies and streams by human activities; the need for effective sewage systems with pure water as a by-product.

Water is a symbolic issue for human survival precisely because of its practical importance in human life as one of the essential 'global commons' gifted to us by nature. The message of *The Well at the World's End* is that we are equal, at the end of the day, not in any externally

---

137. Peter Kropotkin, *Mutual aid: a factor of evolution* (Knopf, 1914), p.9. Reprinted by Freedom Press, 1987

justified sense (either God-given or Inalienable Rights) but in a willed social sense. We determine that we want to live in a society of equals. But that decision is rooted in turn in our knowledge that we are dependent on the natural environment, and in particular on the 'global commons' of clean air, pure water and food. The production of food, in turn, is dependent on access to the land as 'a common treasury for all', as the Diggers yesterday and The Land is Ours today have recognised. We need production for human need rather than profit, the use of farming methods which are sustainable over long periods. Utopian as these understandings may be, they are also deeply rooted in a knowledge of the evil in the world and its people, as made manifest in the century since Morris's death; the pervasiveness of greed and inequality.

There has to be room for difference in the modern world, because it is a precondition of our lives together in communities, but that difference cannot continue to involve the claim for control over undue shares of natural resources. Morris saw around him in Victorian England, the degradation wrought by industrial life. He also saw that it was the greed generated by capitalism, and the moral vacuum that lay at its heart, which threatened civilisation. The case is sound in personal terms within a society, but also in the relation between nations, and particularly with regard to the proportion of the world's resources at present absorbed by the United States of America. In turn, of course, this makes them the biggest producer of pollution too — twenty-two percent of the world's carbon dioxide produced by four percent of its population. This greed is active rather than passive: at the time of the Kyoto conference on global warming in 1997, Anita Pollack, one of three MEPs in the European Union team at Kyoto stated:

The United States... is hooked on big cars, cheap fuel and over-heated and over-cooled buildings. Whilst it could make big efforts with energy saving alone, it has been bought heart and soul by a thirteen million dollar advertising campaign paid for by fossil fuel and motor companies. They brought scientists and a massive public relations team together to convince the US Congress and the American people that the best their great nation can contribute to save the planet is to suggest that they could maybe stabilise their greenhouse gas emissions at 1990 levels by 2012. Al Gore tried to sell this to the conference as a thirty percent reduction on what would happen under business as usual.[138]

In relation to the themes of this book; freedom, yes, because it is the precondition of our humanity; but equality and community too because they are the preconditions of a recognition of how our own survival and that of the planet are interconnected. The individual/society antithesis is an illusion, because without society, without community, without solidarity, there is no individual option any longer. We have the liberty, the technology, to live independently of nature, but only at the frightful cost of the destruction of the global ecosystem. And the agents of that destruction are not faceless people but the employees of multinational companies who want to deny us access to the global commons, and the politicians who sit on their hands rather than act. Direct action, whether it is aimed at fields of genetically modified crops or industrial concerns that pollute our environment, is justified because it represents the long-term interests of the vast majority of the human race.

Morris and Utopia

Georgiana Burne-Jones reported that William Morris died 'as gently, as quietly as a babe who is satisfied drops from its mother's breast'.[139]

---

138. Anita Pollack, 'Is there too much hot air or did Kyoto save the planet?', *New Ground*, no. 54, Spring 1998
139. In Nicholas Salmon, 'A friendship from heaven: Burne-Jones and William Morris's', *Journal of the William Morris Society*, volume 13, no.1, 1998, p.12

> Utopia does not express desire, but enables people to work
> towards an understanding of what is necessary for human
> fulfilment, a broadening, deepening and raising of aspira-
> tions in terms quite different from those of their everyday
> life. (Ruth Levitas)[140]

As Krishan Kumar[141] has pointed out, Morris was provoked into writing *News from Nowhere* by the enormous
irritation he felt at the publication and success of Edward
Bellamy's *Looking Backward*. Morris described it in a letter to John Glasier (13 May 1889) as a 'cockney paradise',
a world in which the worst features of industrial Victorian
Britain were only mitigated by a centrally imposed order
and equality which later critics have found to be a precursor of both National Socialism and State Socialism. As
Kumar rightly suggests, the contrast with Morris is in the
tone, as much as in the content, 'a way of describing the
look of people, and their relation with each other; in a particular sense of nature, as landscape, and as a way and
means of life'.[142]

This question of a Morris 'tone' is crucial for an understanding of the continuing significance and relevance of
Morris for 'how we live and how we might live'. I hope I
have made it clear in my use of Morris material in this
book that it is not a question of taking particular bits of
Morris's writing, particular policies, let alone particular
wallpaper or fabric designs, and importing them into the
public arena of our lives together. It is, rather, an intuitive
issue: a particular way of looking at the world around us,
of thinking about the relationship between people and
nature, the purposes of work, the ethical basis of the good
society: what Jean Saunders described in chapter seven as
'the William Morris in me'. And finally, it is a particular

---

140. Ruth Levitas, *The concept of utopia* (Philip Allan, 1990) p.122
141. Krishan Kumar, *Utopia and anti-utopia in modern times* (Black-
     well, 1987), especially chapter 5, 'Utopia as socialism: Edward Bel-
     lamy and *Looking Backward*'.
142. Kumar, p.161

way of viewing the relationships between people, and the role of love in beginning to fill the silences of the vast, empty universe that the scientists have bequeathed to us. Love that makes sense of the little corners of life, and the little corners of the universe which we inhabit, and in that way, gives meaning to what otherwise would be without meaning.

Morris, then, provoked by Bellamy. And it is to Morris's review of *Looking Backward*, published in *Commonweal* on 22 June 1889, that we turn for the final word on the future:

> It is necessary to point out here that there are some Socialists who do not think that the problem of the organisation of life and necessary labour can be dealt with by a huge national centralisation, working by a kind of magic for which no one feels himself responsible; that on the contrary it will be necessary for the unit of administration to be small enough for every citizen to feel himself responsible for its details, and be interested in them; that individual men cannot shuffle off the business of life on to the shoulders of an abstraction called the State, but must deal with it in conscious association with each other: that variety of life is as much an aim of a true Communism as equality of condition, and that nothing but these two will bring about real freedom... And, finally, that art, using that word in its widest sense and due signification, is not a mere adjunct of life which free and happy men can do without, but the necessary expression and indispensable instrument of human happiness.

The William Morris Society

The life, work and ideas of William Morris are as important today as they were in his lifetime. The William Morris Society exists to make them as widely known as possible.

The many-sidedness of Morris and the variety of his activities bring together in the Society those who are interested in him as designer, craftsman, businessman, poet, socialist, or who admire his robust and generous personality, his creative energy and courage. Morris aimed for a state of affairs in which all might enjoy the potential richness of human life. His thoughts on how we might live, on creative work, leisure and machinery, on ecology and conservation, on the place of the arts in our lives and their relation to politics, as on much else, remain as challenging now as they were in his time. He provides a focus for those who deplore the progressive dehumanization of the world in modern times and who believe, with him, that the trend is not inevitable.

The Society provides information on topics of interest to its members and arranges lectures, visits, exhibitions and other events. It encourages the reprinting of his writings and the continued manufacture of his textile and wallpaper designs. It publishes a journal twice a year, free to members, which carries articles across the field of Morris scholarship. It also publishes a quarterly newsletter giving details of its programme, new publications and other matters of interest concerning Morris and his circle. Members are invited to contribute items both to the journal and to the newsletter. The William Morris Society has a world-wide membership and offers the chance to make contact with fellow Morrisians both in Britain and abroad.

Regular events include a Kelmscott Lecture, a birthday party held in March, and visits to exhibitions and such places as the William Morris Gallery, Red House, Kelmscott Manor and Standen. These visits, our tours and our short residential study courses, enable members living abroad or outside London, to participate in the Society's activities. The Society also has local groups in various parts of Britain and affiliated Societies in the USA and Canada.

For further details, write to:
The Hon. Membership Secretary, Kelmscott House,
26 Upper Mall, Hammersmith, London W6 9TA